Searching for Sycorax

Searching for Sycorax

~

Black Women's Hauntings of
Contemporary Horror

KINITRA D. BROOKS

Rutgers University Press

New Brunswick, Camden, and Newark, New Jersey, and London

978-0-8135-8461-4
978-0-8135-8462-1
978-0-8135-8463-8
978-0-8135-8464-5

Cataloging-in-Publication record for this book is available from the Library of Congress.

A British Cataloging-in-Publication record for this book is available from the British Library.

Lyrics to "Hoodoo Lady" by Memphis Minnie reprinted with permission of the Minnie Lawlers Estate.

∞ The paper used in this publication meets the requirements of the American National Standard for Information Sciences—Permanence of Paper for Printed Library Materials, ANSI Z39.48–1992.

www.rutgersuniversitypress.org

Manufactured in the United States of America

For my parents
Gregory and Wanda
Thank you for so much
This book exists because of you

Contents

Preface

Though mute throughout, she's [Grace Jones] a
powerful presence as vampire queen Katrina.
—Ian Berriman, SFX.com

I can say that I can't think of any one [black woman] that has ever
been an author or illustrator in the genre whatsoever.... It'll happen
eventually, I'm sure. It's just one of those things that hasn't surfaced yet.
—William, attendee at the World Horror Convention 2013

I was a seven-year-old curled up in a movie theater seat watching Ms. Jones as Katrina in *Vamp* (1986). My fingers were curled in anticipation on either side of my head, ready to plug my ears in terror at any hint of surprise or film-constructed danger. I was ensconced between my beloved aunt Errolyn—whom I had convinced that I was old enough to handle horror—and my older cousin Lee—whom I believe had more fun snickering at my reactions to the film than actually watching the movie himself. My eyes were glued to the (then) gargantuan screen at the Joy Theatre in New Orleans, Louisiana—well, at least until a vampire appeared on screen—then they were glued to the recessed lighting in the floor. My imagination began to ponder the space behind those lights, calculating if it was big enough for a vampire's hand to fit through and grab my leg. I watched the film in a semicatatonic state of a terror I had never felt before, hoping, wishing, and praying that it would just END! I was so proud of myself and

I sighed with relief as the credits begin to roll—I had survived! And then my aunt Errolyn tore my world asunder as she announced that since she'd enjoyed the movie so much we were going to stick around for the next showing! I died a little inside as I collapsed into my seat ready to endure another round of torture, and Lee collapsed into another round of raucous laughter at my expense.

I now recognize the genius of my aunt Errolyn and appreciate the gift she gave me that day, the gift of an intellectual curiosity about horror. It was the second showing that gave me the bravery to truly *look* at the film, as I now had the ability to move beyond my terror and began to enjoy the movie and become enraptured by the dark beauty of Grace Jones.[1] And though I loved Katrina, my young mind had a strong sense that there was something wrong with Grace Jones's distinctive beauty ultimately being portrayed as a horrific vampire, that her features became exaggerated and monstrously ugly when she finally revealed her "true" self. I also began to wonder, why the heck didn't she talk?[2] Was her character mute? Even at seven years old I could see the need to communicate in those eerily colored eyes in the midst of her painted face and wondered, why didn't they let her *talk*? Why was she silenced? I would eventually learn that the word for which I was searching for Katrina's characterization was "problematic."

My active little mind began to wonder if there were there other central black female characters in horror movies that were not painted so scarily. And, even more important, were there cool black girl characters that kicked the monster's butt and got the cute guy in the end? As I grew older, my aunt Errolyn and aunt Linda introduced me to Jamie Lee Curtis's Laurie from *Halloween* (1978) and Kim from *Prom Night* (1980) and other cool girls who kicked butt and sometimes got a cute boyfriend in the end. Yet I began to realize that the girl was always white. And after a somewhat traumatic introduction to zombies revealed even more about my growing love for horror: we black girls were absent—we were never there![3]

As I grew older, I gained a love of literature from my mother and a love of genre fiction from my father. My lived experience

FIG. 1. Grace Jones as Katrina, *Vamp* (1986).

as a young black woman continuously highlighted the erasure of black women in mainstream horror. I began to ask questions as my consumption of genre media increased in my late teens. Why were there never any black people in Sunnydale, California? And was I the only one who thought the Chinese slayer (Ming Qiu) and the Afroed blaxploitation slayer (April Weeden) from the season five episode of *A Fool for Love* were far more interesting in their fleeting minutes onscreen than Buffy Anne Summers (Sarah Michelle Gellar) had been throughout seven seasons of *Buffy the Vampire Slayer* (1997–2003)? Did Jada Pinkett's character, Maureen, and Elise Neal's Hallie both have to die in *Scream 2* (1997)? And why, in my absolute favorite subgenre of horror—the zombie apocalypse—were there never any black women in the group of survivors? Hell, there weren't ever *any* women of color— no Puerto Ricans, no Koreans, no Chicanas, no Pakistanis—none of the many different shades and incarnations of womanhood I encountered on a daily basis. It was a blatant erasure that began to seriously bother me, which then became an irritation and finally developed into a rash for which I needed to find a healing salve in order to save my love for horror.

I questioned if it was possible for mainstream horror to construct complicated black women characters. In my early twenties I began to see flashes of hope with the release of films such as *Supernova* (2002), *AVP: Alien vs. Predator* (2004), and *28 Days Later* (2002) and found joy in horror films' recognition that the black girl can survive in the end—and if she's lucky, she gets to hang out with The Predator along the way![4] It was as a graduate student that I fell hard for Michonne, a kick-ass black female character in Robert Kirkman's ongoing comic zombie opus *The Walking Dead* (2003–), and Selena, who righteously slayed the infected with her handy machete from Danny Boyle's kinetic homage to the zombie apocalypse, *28 Days Later*.[5] Both characters were capable black women who actively contributed to their own survival. They were often portrayed as protectors of the group without being a piously perfect caretaker as many black female characters in mainstream movies are wont to be. Had mainstream horror begun to construct complicated black women characters?

And then I watched/read both texts for a second time—and that word, "problematic," popped up again. The characters started out as capable, but then often became a workhorse of the group. The white female characters were vulnerable, protected, and even rescued in heroic feats of grandeur by the men in the group. Why didn't anyone ever rescue the black woman? Why did she always have to rescue herself? Didn't anyone care if she survived? And then I came upon the rape of Michonne and got angry.[6] Tears of anger began to flow as I read each panel while Michonne was brutally beaten and gang-raped by a rival faction of survivors. My eyes froze on one particular panel in which Michonne is framed against a stone wall dressed in nothing but a ripped T-shirt. Her bruised and swollen face bespoke the sexual and physical violence she had just endured in her nudity. The only thing that prevents her from collapsing in a heap of trauma is that she is chained to the wall by a pair of slave shackles trapping her wrists. That panel represented so much pain, horror, and trauma experienced by the black women I studied as a student of black feminist literature— my sense of self demanded I do something.

I became transfixed on finding more complex characterizations of black women in horror *created* by black women. I began by diving into Tananarive Due's African Immortals series and reveling in complex black characters as she Africanized the European vampire. I began rooting for the survival of the supernatural power couple Damali Richards and Carlos Riviera as LA Banks reworked, reimagined, and significantly improved upon the legend of the young girl chosen to protect the world by slaying vampires.[7] I still hungered for more than black women's interpretation of vampires; I wanted to read our takes on zombies, ghosts, and the supernatural in religion.

The inclusion of black women in critical horror studies is paramount because of the unique positionality of black women, most specifically manifested in the simultaneity of oppressions that aids in defining black women's identities. Postmodern horror studies' problematic focus on questions of monstrosity regarding white women and black men has proven detrimental to its own saliency and relevance—the critical study of black women within the genre is a volley against mainstream horror's willful ignorance of the intersections of identity that composes its audience and, more important, its expanding pool of creators. It is important that black women be complexly presented as both characters and creators of the horror genre.

This project is a search and rescue mission. I aim to find the black women in contemporary horror and critique the complex ways in which they manifest as characters, as creators, and as rebels to the conventions of both horror theory and black feminist theory. This text openly defies the mistaken notion—as articulated by William in the epigraph—that black women horror creators do not exist or are so miniscule as to be rendered insignificant to the genre. I make visible the black woman's significance, relevance, and subversion to conventional horror theories and narratives.

I end my investigation with the black woman creators' challenge that horror adapts or dies—as they are examples of the growing demographic changes that the horror genre must pursue and develop to continue its deep cultural influences.

Acknowledgments

I have been writing this book for the better part of a decade and I want to take this opportunity to thank everyone who brought this moment to fruition. I would first and foremost like to thank God, for none of this would be possible without my faith and the protection He provides through my ancestors. I am so thankful for my sisters, Cincia Kerr who keeps me sane and grounded and Kelsi Brooks, who shows me how to chase my dreams. My brother-in-law, Solanke Kerr and the best niece and nephew a woman could ask for, Isabella Marie and Gregory Elijah. My aunts, Clara Stansberry, Earline Brooks, and Sedonia Brooks, for their steady guidance as well as my awesomely cool Uncle Raymond Dunn. I would also like to thank my cousin, Sergeant First Class Retired Leonidas Brooks for letting me share memories of our beloved Aunt Errolyn and his mom, my Aunt Linda. And to the rest of the Diva Trinity—We made it, Drs. Brandy Huderson and Ashley Jackson!

I have been blessed with an amazing network of girlfriends while here in San Antonio. These women have become my family and have always been there for me when I dared doubt my abilities. So thank you, Sonja Lanehart, Joycelyn Moody, Deborah Thoma, LaGuana Gray, Rhonda Gonzales, Patricia Francois, Andrea "Vocab" Sanderson, Kirsten Thompson, and Kellie Hamilton Ferrier. And I also thank your partners and children for welcoming me into their hearts and homes.

When I was at my lowest point in writing this book, I met John Jennings who invited me to *Astroblackness 2* and informally inducted me into the Black Speculative Arts Movement—or did I just bumrush and make a place for myself? Meeting and connecting with a group of black academics who were geeked out by all things blerd gave me that final push of confidence to ascertain that my theories had a place in the academy and were urgently needed. Thank you for being #Squad John, Susana Morris, Stacey Robinson, Regina Bradley, Reynaldo Anderson, and Nalo Hopkinson.

Thank you to my trove of mentors who have guided my career; I must commend their guidance, beginning with Trudier Harris who continues to pick up the phone whenever I need her. I would also like to thank Gwendolyn Pough, Michele Levy, Mae G. Henderson, and Nicholas Jones for their continued support and belief in my potential.

I would like to thank the University of Texas at San Antonio, particularly the support provided by the College of Liberal and Fine Arts Faculty Development Leave program—please bring it back. That semester of research without any teaching commitments proved invaluable to finishing my monograph, and other professors need that support. I am thankful for the Faculty Boot Camp at the National Center for Faculty Development Diversity—my working group helped me develop the discipline and rigor needed to finish this book project. I would also like to thank the Sue E. Denman Distinguished Chair in American Literature for welcoming me as a postdoctoral fellow and the Brackenridge Endowed Chair in Literature and the Humanities for continuous research support.

I received so much help from my graduate students in terms of gathering and organizing my research. Thank you, Stephanie Schoellman, for your help with the Appendix; Christopher Guzman for helping me with the book's visuals; and Alexis McGee, for your dedication.

Finally, I want to thank my husband, Amadou Jallow, for being my anchor.

Searching for Sycorax

Introduction
Searching for Sycorax
Black Women and Horror

Hast thou forgot the foul witch Sycorax ... hast thou forgot her?
—*The Tempest,* Act I, Scene II

Defining the genre of horror remains an ongoing challenge, for it is one of the few genres that depends upon the reaction of the viewer/reader.[1] Like many questions of genre, particularly concerning genres not traditionally considered the High Arts, producing a definitive taxonomic definition of horror proves quite difficult. Contemporary horror fiction is a space in which deep-seated human anxieties can be given free reign because we are often defined by that which terrifies us. Our cultures and our lives are founded upon preventing a confrontation with our terrors. We create governments and prisons to civilize ourselves and abate our fear of anarchy and mankind's potential for savagery. We throw money at science to ameliorate our dis-ease, with the hegemony operating on the assumption that science can and will solve everything—disease, famine, war, and so forth. The Western hegemony loves binaries—the world is defined by what is good or evil, living or dead, black or white, male or female. Yet postmodern horror is a world in which there is an "absolute blurring of boundaries between good AND evil, real AND unreal. . . . Institutions are questioned and the master status of the universal (read male, white, moneyed, heterosexual) subject deteriorates."[2] Most contemporary horror critics—including this critic—center their studies on a differing amalgamation of the horror definitions found in leading genre theorists, such as Isabel Cristina Piñedo, Noël Carroll, and Robin Wood. It is necessary to note that *Searching for Sycorax* is not an attempt to redefine the definition of horror, but simply to refine the projects of these genre theorists in order to present a contemporary definition of horror that allows for an analysis of how black women "worry the lines" of the supposedly inclusive nature of horror theory.[3] I also aim to propagate my insistence that horror must allow a space for black womanhood, even as it has casually overlooked black women in its past iterations. Contemporary horror theory and black feminist literary theory can and must continue to expand and adapt to their rapidly changing audiences for both continued survival and relevancy—for black women creators are actively revising and redefining the genre of horror.

Isabel Cristina Piñedo makes an important contribution to horror studies by contemporizing the genre by offering a racially gendered critique. Piñedo outlines three characteristics of postmodern horror that I read through Zack Snyder's remake of *Dawn of the Dead* (2008). The first characteristic presents a violent disruption with the everyday world; the second characteristic portrays a horror that transgresses and violates boundaries; and the final characteristic questions the validity of rationalism.

Postmodern horror begins with a violent disruption with the everyday world.[4] Early in the film, Ana, the lead character, rushes out of her house and stands in the driveway as the camera does a slow 180-degree pan to the right. We see the devastation and chaos: a woman in her nightgown is chased and bitten by a zombie; another neighbor, this time in a priest's collar, shoots a zombie on his lawn and demands that Ana stays back via gunpoint. Finally, as he crosses the street moving toward her—gun still aloft—to see if she is human, his body suddenly crumples and careens off screen as he is hit by an ambulance gone out of control. The viewer is drawn to conclude that this ambulance has an attacking zombie inside. Ana has entered a world that privileges gore, "the explicit dismemberment, evisceration, putrefication and myriad other forms of boundary violations with copious amounts of blood."[5] In a previous scene, Ana watches her husband, Luis, become a zombie before our very eyes. Ana, a nurse, rescues her husband from the zombified little girl next door, Vivian, who has bitten him in the neck. In the bedroom, they both struggle to put pressure on the geyser of blood that is his neck wound. Blood spews everywhere, on Ana, Luis, and the bed, as Luis slowly succumbs to his wounds. In shock, Ana wanders to her bedroom window, distracted by sounds of distress. The screen shot shows Ana, clearly focused in the foreground as her husband slowly rises to join the wake of the undead in the blurry haze of the shot's background. Suddenly, there is a rack to focus upon Luis as he initiates a screaming attack and jumps toward her. They engage, sloppily, as zombie Luis cannot hold on to her because of the slipperiness of his own blood smeared across her body. She escapes to the bathroom, slamming the door shut as she crashes into the porcelain tub. These scenes portray a thematic and visual blurring of the boundaries between Western binaries—such as life/death, good/evil, moral/immoral, all taking place at dawn, that special time between night and day.

This blurring leads to the second characteristic of the postmodern horror genre—the portrayal of a horror that transgresses and violates boundaries. The existence of a reality populated by zombies demonstrates humanity's anxieties about the "impermeability of death."[6] Zack Snyder's rotting zombies violate the staid boundaries between life and death, while also preying upon our anxieties about contagion. Vivian bites Luis, even as Ana notices something peculiar about the tween and firmly tells her to stay back. Ana finally slams and locks the bedroom door, but it is too late, for the contagion has already entered the sanctity of her bedroom—through Luis's infected bite. Throughout the film, the viewer is reminded that the bite of the zombie is infectious and initiates a painful (and sometimes long) transformation of the human body into another walking rotting corpse. The zombie infection plays upon contemporary fears of infectious diseases such as Ebola, HIV/AIDS, and swine flu. The zombie infection also plays upon the racialized nature of contagion as seen with the racist "dog-whistles" that accompanied Western fears of swine flu (China) and Ebola as well as HIV/AIDS (Africa).

As Piñedo contends, the final characteristic of postmodern horror is that the genre questions the validity of rationality.[7] The science of the Western world is diminished and is often the cause of the dangers that zombification presents to humanity. The characters that survive these fictions adapt quickly, relying on human ingenuity and intuition paired with preindustrial weapons such as machetes, baseball bats, hammers, katanas, and revolvers. Piñedo insists: "horror exposes the limits of rationality and compels us to confront the irrational . . . [particularly] the disordered, ineffable, chaotic, and unpredictable universe which constitutes the underside of life."[8] In this horrific world of gore, in which "the narrative is propelled by violence," the characterizations studied in this project are established and analyzed.[9] These characteristics relate to my contention that even as the horror genre subverts and perverts classic hegemonic tenets, it remains dangerously staid in its supplication to weary racial and gender dynamics that constricts its revolutionary potential for cultural repudiation.

Noël Carroll presents an incredibly thorough attempt to define and create a philosophy of horror even as he preempts arguments against his very definition. Carroll's work, *The Philosophy of Horror or Paradoxes of the Heart* (1990), remains a staple of critical horror theory, even over twenty years after its publication, because he muses upon the topic of horror with sobering respect, offering a rational and deductive contemplation upon defining horror. Carroll juxtaposes his theory, what he calls "art-horror," against other interpretations of horror—those associated with the horrors people inflict upon each other—such as enslavement, rape, and war. Art-horror is distinguished as the constructed creativity of what our society refers to when it speaks of horror as related to books, films, and television.[10] Carroll spends much of his first chapter distinguishing what horror is not and craftily delineating it from its popular conflation with both the science fiction and fantasy genres.[11]

Carroll defines art-horror as an emotion of fear instigated by the simultaneity of threat and disgust.[12] The reader feels threatened by anything that elicits fear, be it moral, physical, psychological, social, and/or cognitive; yet Carroll is the first to acknowledge that many things elicit fear. He insists that the important interlocutor for art-horror occurs when that thing also joins with the disgust elicited by impurity, something that is categorically interstitial, incomplete, and/or formless.[13] I highlight the disgust of impurity because it recurs in my analysis of the categorical interstitiality of black women in horror.

In defining horror, I choose to privilege Robin Wood's definition of horror: "[It is] when Normality is threatened by The Monster . . . [or The Other]."[14] This definition works even as it proves overly simplistic and broad. The infusion of Piñedo and Carroll adds complexity and specificity. It is necessary to note that all of these critics agree that horror, like most other genres, is a textual category for discovering and developing larger societal anxieties through certain themes of disquieting interstitialities often referred to as monsters. In the end, my project is not to define horror, which is an ongoing conversation, but to interrogate its problematic themes of racially gendered subjects and creators—specifically black women.

The remake of *Dawn of the Dead* was simultaneously critically admired and panned. Many genre purists cringed at Zack Snyder's decision to use fast zombies who could run after their prey even as other critics enjoyed the thrilling ride of an updated homage to George Romero's classic 1978 study of Western materialism.[15] Ultimately, the film's supporters won out over its detractors, as the film has proven popular within the latest zombie criticisms.[16] Though this remake broke from classic zombie tropes in many ways and may even be read as a criticism of that tradition, it still remains true to certain distinctive features typical of contemporary horror, the absence of black women. The film continues the problematic tradition of the (non)representation of certain intersections of race and gender in Western film and literature. Using multiple texts, I begin *Searching for Sycorax* by interrogating how patriarchal and Eurocentric notions perpetuate multiracial representations of men while perpetuating monoracial representations of women in contemporary horror, underscoring the challenges such portrayals represent for black women characters and creators.

Dawn of the Dead has some racial diversity, with not one but *two* significant characters of color.[17] African American actors Ving Rhames and Mekhi Phifer depict the characters of Kenneth and Andre, respectively. Furthermore, director Zack Snyder's pairing of Phifer's Andre with Inna Korobkina's Luda (who plays his pregnant Russian girlfriend) can certainly be read as his enduring statement on the progressive nature of Hollywood's stance on the power of love in interracial coupledom, even in the postapocalyptic dystopia of zombies. Though Snyder revamps and extends the zombie trope of the cool, calm, and collected black male survivor and ultimate leader of the group, he fails to extend these courtesies of presence and complexity of characterization to women of color.[18] In the film, Snyder offers a variety of representations of (white) womanhood ranging from competent to incompetent—from Sarah Polley's portrayal of the adept survivor, Ana, to Lindy Booth's characterization of the useless sexual distraction, Nicole. The film even portrays a range of ages, from Jayne Eastwood's knowledgeable elder, Norma, to Kim Poirier's naive ingénue, Monica. Snyder reimagines his constructions of white femininity in a solid attempt to show the competence and success of various female survivors subverting the catatonia experienced by Judith O'Dea's Barbra in George Romero's zombie classic, *Night of the Living Dead* (1968).[19] Yet Snyder's exclusion of black women exemplifies contemporary horror's gendered racism by highlighting the absence of black women both onscreen and off.

I focus on this tendency toward exclusion as a tradition, for the problematic lack of representation of women of color in popular Western texts has been systematically analyzed and reproached in the latter half of the twentieth century. Snyder's horror film is not the first text to problematically erase the presence of black women, and it certainly won't be the last. I trace the explicit invisibility of black women to the early seventh century, where basic precepts for

FIG. 2. Mekhi Phifer as Andre and Inna Korobkina as Luda, *Dawn of the Dead* (2004).

modern Western art were actively forming.[20] Sylvia Wynter, in her essay "Beyond Miranda's Meanings: Un/Silencing The 'Demonic Ground' of Caliban's 'Woman,'" critiques William Shakespeare's *The Tempest* (1610) as a text with multiple critically interesting representations of manhood. The characterizations of Prospero, Caliban, Ferdinand, Stephano, and Trinculo demonstrate this predisposition by portraying multiple iterations of being white and black, rural and urban, upper-class and lower-class. Wynter suggests that the most significant idea of the play is the critical and cultural implications that the only representation of legitimate womanhood, Miranda, remains a bastion of upper-class whiteness, as the woman of color, Sycorax—the island's first inhabitant—is erased.[21] Yet Sycorax refuses to be excluded, as her absence in erasure is subverted by her presence as an idea that produces fear and suspicion in the play's remaining characters.

I employ the language of cultural critic bell hooks and describe Sycorax's position as an "absent presence."[22] Her formerly physical incarnation of previously carnal existence touches most characters on the island—she gave Caliban life, trapped Ariel, and is a recently deceased occupier and power broker of the very island that manifests Prospero's power.[23] Though her physical body has surrendered, Sycorax is present without the need for either a body or a voice; *The Tempest* falsely assumes her self-actualization is not necessary, for her presence is only felt through others' construction of her. The assumption that Sycorax no longer matters shatters with Prospero's emphatic warning that her dark presence and power are only forgotten by the insolent, as he demands: "Hast thou forgot the foul witch Sycorax . . . hast thou forgot her?"[24] Sycorax's corporeal death has magnified her subversive presence, haunting multiple plot points and its participants. Sycorax is now a hant—or ghost—that remains spiritually and psychologically present and powerful.

The problematic characterization of Sycorax mirrors the quandary of black women in contemporary horror. It is the absent presence of black women in the horror genre that imbues my search for Sycorax—that is, black women in horror—as I investigate her presence in novels, short fiction, comic books, and film. It is my contention that Sycorax is incorrectly considered absent, moot, an apparition that only haunts nutty liberal professors obsessed with horror. This text demonstrates the subversive presence of black women in horror through a critical analysis of incarnations in the genre.

I begin by exploring her characterizations in horror texts. I insist that black women horror characters are plagued by their construction as a mistreated tool used to further the more careful and considerate construction of other characters. The textual reality of the black woman's presence highlights the misreading of Robin Wood's horror formula.[25] This is problematic because the majority of the critical and textual exploration of horror centers on the normative experiences of white men; therefore, the anxiety examined in horror is continuously about the other sides of the white male binary.[26] This penchant actively excludes the black woman, for she is the non-Other, the Other of the white male's Others (black men and white women). The absence is found in the lack of agency given to the black women horror constructs examined in this text's first chapter. They are present in the narrative but problematically so because their existence is predicated on buttressing the narrative development of other non-black woman characters.

I continue my mission by exposing Sycorax's absent presence in the most unlikely of environs—black feminist literary theory.

I explore how the black feminist project of marking and connecting black women's literature to the High Arts—an important revision of the *Belles Lettres*—actively excludes specific types of women's writing and applicable theories for reading classic black feminist literature. A significant portion of black women's literature is marginalized, particularly genre fiction—and for my particular area of research, horror fiction. This area of the project presents a historical context for contemporary black women horror texts by connecting their work with the substantial elements of horror found in classic black women's literature. I insist upon removing the necessity for the pairing absence from Sycorax's presence. These elements have often been misnamed and associated with popularly accepted theoretical frameworks such as magical realism and trauma theory. In too many instances, horror texts have been subject to the privileging of the horror of trauma above the specific genre of horror.

Next, I lay a theoretical foundation for recognizing Sycorax's presence in black women's contemporary literature. I originate a syncretic theoretical framework that is specifically black *and* female—for the texts of these creators reflect the racially gendered simultaneity of oppressions that plague black womanhood as well as the blurring of the genres of speculative fiction. I adopt the tenets of black feminist theory and contemporary genre theory to term how black women purposely obfuscate the lines between science fiction, fantasy, and horror to deliver a fluid fiction that grounds itself in traditional African religious practices and epistemes. The realization of fluid fiction aids in black women genre writers articulating a radical black literary subjectivity that centers black women.

My fourth and final exploration of Sycorax is to develop a black women's aesthetic of horror through the framework of folkloric horror that centers African diasporic women's spirituality in its origination. I engage this syncretism to subvert mainstream horror's willful blindness to Sycorax's presence. I explore Sycorax's presence in what is considered classic black women's literature and through the tenets of the framework even as I later insist that innovative black women horror writers artfully subvert its elements by incorporating contemporary horror tropes such as zombies and demons. Finally, I read folkloric horror in black women's music and performativity as I demonstrate their intentional embodiment and conflation of the blueswoman and the conjure woman.

Sycorax Haunts Horror

My critical interests have been piqued by the realization of how a startling majority of contemporary horror texts, authors, and the subsequent critical theory that outlines and interrogates the genre sustain the idea noted by Gloria T. Hull in 1982 that "all the women are white, and all the blacks are men."[27] The project of recovering Sycorax remains urgent because the intersecting identities of black women represent and illuminate the weaknesses in contemporary horror criticism. It is in the works of critics such as Carol Clover, Isabel Cristina Piñedo, Natasha Patterson, and Stephen Harper that the interrogation of horror demonstrates a problematic cleaving of black women's identities by dividing their analysis into ones that examine race *or* gender—with only a growing few, Harry Benshoff and Robin R. Coleman-Means, critiquing the intersections of both. It is here that I enter to continue the inclusion and analysis of black women characters in horror texts and the unique positionality of racially gendered constructions and how their situatedness interrogates and subverts the normativity of whiteness in feminist horror theory and the normativity of maleness in black monstrosity theory. Furthermore, the construction of theories of horror must become applicable to both the characterizations of black women and black women horror creators. This more nuanced theorization would serve to strengthen horror studies as a whole and act as a template for future critiques that include the multiple intersections of racially gendered horror constructions. As noted above, I am certainly not the first critic to notice the fleeting apparitions of black women in horror. But *Searching for Sycorax* moves beyond the necessary brevity of book chapters and journal articles to produce the first sustained critical examination of black women in contemporary horror.

From my analysis of black women characters' diminished subjectivity and/or outsized corporeal or emotional strength in contemporary horror and genre fiction, I conclude the stakes are these: such stereotypical portraits will impact real black women by failing to acknowledge the complications their situatedness brings to feminism, critical race theory, and Western society as a whole. The ignorance regarding black women's unique positionality particularly subverts the dominant memes of mainstream feminism's fight for displays of strength and the ability to work beside men.[28] The same ignorance subverts the dominance of black critical theory's focus upon centralizing the black male's demands for power and structural change. When black women themselves construct more realistic portraits of black female characters, the risks, stakes, or effects are a more holistic and inclusive depiction of the lived realities of black womanhood. Furthermore, it is in the best interest of the horror genre and its surrounding industries to initiate more profound efforts at inclusion. Its formerly ideal customer base—white, heterosexual, middle-class young males—can no longer sustain its development even as those people outside of the ideal demand more representation. Its potential for survival by expansion must be rooted in the exploration of other races, sexualities, class statuses, and females—identities and intersections whose disposable incomes must be tapped into. The inclusion of black women and the many intersections they represent acts as a shifting signifier that constitutes such a cross section of poststructural identities that the critical analysis of black women reflects the critical realities of all other peoples.[29]

Black Feminist Theory and Horror

I engage the aforementioned ideas of horror to question Sycorax's exclusion and marginalized status in an already ghettoized genre that is held in such disdain. The significance of my project is four-pronged. First, I address what bell hooks refers to as film's "violent erasure of black womanhood" by expanding hooks's black feminist theory of the oppositional gaze to include a horror framework.

I examine contemporary horror fiction as a product of the psychological anxieties associated with black women. These anxieties act as an interlocutor between historical constructions of Negrophobia and Gynophobia resulting in a construction of black female characters grounded in the controlling image of the strong black woman. I contend that this stereotype is employed to suppress the complexities of black women's characterizations in horror, for her black body is often surrendered to the privileging of complicating non-black and/or non-female characters. I argue for horror to move beyond stereotypes and demonstrate the revolutionary inclusion rendered when black female characters are complicated.

Second, I articulate a space to examine horror texts and black feminist literature through horror frameworks even as I challenge black feminist theory's previous unwillingness to do so. I establish a literary and theoretical history for the writers and their texts that I explore in the second half of the text. Next, I present a deep revision of what is currently referred to as black women's speculative fiction. I insist it is a misnomer and explicate an ideal that elucidates black women's purposeful blending of the genres of science fiction, fantasy, and horror, which I term fluid fiction. I suggest that black women genre writers employ fluid fiction to achieve a radical black female subjectivity that openly challenges the exhausted doctrines of genre fiction. Finally, I present an articulation of folkloric horror, a black women horror aesthetic theory that explicates how the texts of black women horror creators revise and reimagine African diasporic folklore as a mode of participating in and interrogating contemporary mainstream horror.[30]

Black women have slowly and painfully been developing as more significant characters in horror texts since the last quarter of the twentieth century, yet their constructions continue to sacrifice their subjectivity in order to privilege their a/object difference. The problematic nature of black women's horror constructions has been most visible in film and media—though I would posit Grendel's mother from *Beowulf* and the aforementioned Sycorax as early iterations of monstrous black women literary characters. In her foundational volume *Horror Noire: Black in American Horror Films from the 1890s to Present* (2011), Robin R. Means Coleman denotes that blacks in early films were portrayed as "odd and primitive" with notable characterizations "as savage, deadly natives."[31] These stereotypes were eventually exacerbated in subsequent horror films as horror coalesced into a specific film genre in the 1930s. Many of these resulted in blacks being associated with voodoo—what critic Ashlee Blackwell refers to as "voodoo horror" in which all the roles for black women were "embedded with the idea that black women use voodoo as a retaliation against whites."[32] Blackwell lists filmic examples such as *Chloe, Love is Calling You* (1934), *Ouanga* (1936), and *King of the Zombies* (1941).[33]

Moving forward, there are few examples of black women in horror films until we arrive at what critic Harry Benshoff refers to as Blaxploitation horror, which included films such as *Blacula* (1972), *Scream Blacula Scream* (1973), *Abby* (1974), and *Sugar Hill* (1974). Each film contained central black women characters, but the majority embodied what Coleman refers to as the "Enduring Woman," which describes the black women horror characters of this era as "soldiers in ongoing battles of discrimination, in which total victory is elusive."[34] Too often, the boogeymen in these films were differing manifestations of the racialized sexism and "corruption" faced by black urban women of the time.[35] It is clear that even as the presence of black women in horror films has grown, until recently there has been a distinct failure in the development of complex characterizations of black women. It is here, in the growing negotiated autonomy of black women in horror, that the four chapters of this project dwell.[36]

The first chapter, "The Importance of Neglected Intersections: Characterizations of Black Women in Horror Texts," examines the problematic nonmonstrous character constructions found in the paucity of black female characters that do exist in horror. I suggest that construction of these nonmonstrous characters stems from the belief in and the perpetuation of the stigmatype[37] of the strong black woman that objectifies and allows for a racially gendered removal/framework that distances and distorts the identificatory potential of the ideal viewer. I read Michonne from Robert

Kirkman's comic book series *The Walking Dead* (2003) and Selena from Danny Boyle's *28 Days Later* (2002) as I determine how and why these characters are continually Othered, even as central characters of the narrative.

In a powerfully short blog post celebrating black women in horror, poet Linda Addison traces the origins of the very first appearance of horror in black literature.[38] Addison encounters what she considers the origin of black horror in the folktales found in *Every Tongue Got to Confess* (2001), a collection of stories painstakingly recorded—in early twentieth-century southern black dialect—by the then budding anthropologist Zora Neale Hurston: "Besides themes of religion, family and other social concepts I also found two sections named: 'Devil Tales' and 'Witch and Hant Tales' (Hant means 'haunt' or 'ghost')."[39] Hurston's work highlights black interest in horror as a long-established reality in its communal literature—the rich oral folk culture and tales passed down through familial generations, for Bonnie Barthold insists that "the teller of tales [is] no less than the contemporary novelist."[40]

The most significant critical inquiry of this project demonstrates and analyzes how black women creators are fighting this erasure by re-creating a genre that speaks to their experience even as it subverts dominant horror themes steeped in its contemporary hegemonic discourse. The second chapter, "Black Feminism and the Struggle for Literary Respectability," generates a history of black feminist literary theory and the paucity of past discussions of genre fiction—specifically horror. I insist that in the battle to bring black women's literature into the Canon, speculative texts were sacrificed in order to achieve literary respectability. The third chapter, "Black Women Writing Fluid Fiction: An Open Challenge to Genre Normativity," expands upon the problems of defining genre fiction I explored earlier in this chapter. I dissect the somewhat vague distinctions between the genres of science fiction, fantasy, and horror by employing well-known examples of each genre. The chapter also explores the multiple definitions of speculative fiction and how the term increases the imprecise nature of defining these popular genres. Finally, I present a literary framework termed "fluid fiction" that allows black women genre writers to oscillate between the genres of science fiction, fantasy, and horror, leading to a radically liberatory act that hews space for racially gendered genre fiction. The final chapter, "Folkloric Horror: A New Way of Reading Black Women's Creative Horror," moves toward a black woman's horror aesthetic that privileges self-articulation even as it challenges dominant readings of black womanhood. I compose a specifically black and female horror aesthetic, "folkloric horror," that demonstrates how black women horror writers have grounded their aesthetic in the traditional religious practices of Africa and privilege the realization of the black spiritual feminine. I begin with the reading of two classic black feminist texts, Gloria Naylor's *Mama Day* (1988) and Erna Brodber's *Louisiana* (1994), through the folkloric horror framework. I continue by analyzing the works of contemporary black women horror texts, Chesya Burke's tale "Chocolate Park" (2004) and Kiini Ibura Salaam's short story "Rosamojo" (2003), to demonstrate how they begin to subvert the elements of folkloric horror by incorporating revised horror tropes. I end the chapter by expanding folkloric horror to the music performances of Memphis Minnie and Nina Simone in which I suggest they are simultaneously embodying and subverting the constructs of the blueswoman and the conjure woman. In the search for Sycorax, this project reveals that she rescues herself—and can be found in the works of a growing body of contemporary black women horror writers.

1

The Importance of Neglected Intersections

Characterizations of Black Women in Mainstream Horror Texts

All the women are white, all the blacks are men, but some of us are brave.
—Gloria T. Hull, Patricia Bell Scott, and Barbara Smith

Not only will I stare. I want my look to change reality.
—bell hooks

In June 2005, black feminist critics Yolanda Hood and Gwendolyn D. Pough edited an issue of the *Femspec* journal dedicated to black women and speculative fiction in which they questioned the "surge in fantastic representations of Black womanhood."[1] The critics were the first to make a scholarly note of how black women appeared to be integral characters in the resurgent popularity of genre texts in popular culture. A cursory perusal of postmillennial characterizations in horror reveals a fruitful presence of significant black women in Hollywood—from Angela Basset's protagonist in *Supernova* (2000), to Naomie Harris in *28 Days Later* (2002), to Sanaa Lathan in *AVP: Alien vs. Predator* (2004), to Jessica Lucas in *Evil Dead* (2013). The numbers expand when black women are counted beyond the central role, as seen in the supporting performances of Kelly Rowland in *Freddy vs. Jason* (2003) and Elise Neal and Jada Pinkett Smith in *Scream 2* (1997). Television has quickly followed suit with its sudden realization that serialized horror—when done well—results in astronomical advertising revenues and also features several black women actors, such as Gina Torres as Jasmine in season four of *Angel* (1999–2004) and Bella Crawford in *Hannibal* (2013–2015), Rutina Wesley's Tara Thornton in *True Blood* (2008–2014), Kat Graham as Bonnie Bennett in *The Vampire Diaries* (2009–), Danai Gurira as Michonne and Sonequa Martin-Green as Sasha in *The Walking Dead* (2010–), Necole Beharie as Lt. Abbie Mills in *Sleepy Hollow* (2013–2017), and Halle Berry as Molly Woods in *Extant* (2014–2015). Comic books prove to be light years ahead of sustained characterizations of black women, most popularly Michonne from Robert Kirkman's ongoing comic opus *The Walking Dead* (2003–), Mira Nygus in Atsushi Ōkubo's manga *Soul Eaters* (2004–2013), as well as Yoruichi Shihōin of Tite Kubo's manga Bleach series (2001–).[2] Still, the growing number of black women characters in popular horror culture fails to account for the problematic nature of their constructions.

This chapter exposes mainstream horror's simplistic characterizations of black women by examining their presence in one of horror's most celebrated subgenres, the postapocalyptic zombie text. The zombie text works as an entrance to black women's characterizations in horror for multiple reasons. It is an easily definable horror genre in which there are multiple iterations of black womanhood to explore. Even as the number of black women characters in horror has steadily increased, the manifestations have been incredibly disparate, from entering previously established horror franchises—Aliens, Predator, and Scream—to science fiction horror such as *Supernova* and a television series centered on cannibalistic serial killers, *Hannibal*. This is a good problem to have, but in clearing a space for black women horror characterizations outside of the monstrous, the postapocalyptic zombie text proves the most cohesive as well as the most fruitful. Exposing horror's historically

FIG. 3. Clockwise from top left: Angela Bassett as Dr. Kaela Evers, *Supernova* (2000); Kelly Rowland as Kia Waterson, *Freddy vs. Jason* (2003); Sanaa Lathan as Alexa Woods, *AVP: Alien vs. Predator* (2004); Jada Pinkett Smith as Maureen, *Scream 2* (1997); Jessica Lucas as Olivia, *Evil Dead* (2013); and Rutina Wesley as Tara Thornton, *True Blood* (2008).

unbridled themes of Gynophobia and Negrophobia reveals the dangerously simplistic notion that the presence of black women is enough. My intervention operates within the black feminist framework of the "oppositional gaze" that demands more complex characterizations and grounds my later arguments for the self-articulation of black women in horror. The power of the oppositional gaze acts as a powerful framework in horror by analyzing the black women characters in Robert Kirkman's *The Walking Dead* comic book series (2003–) and Danny Boyle's *28 Days Later* (2002).

All the Women Are White

Fascinating work concerning gender continues within critical studies of horror, but even after thirty years this work has often proven inattentive to the intersections of race, failing to examine its own privileging of whiteness. In *Men, Women and Chainsaws: Gender in the Modern Horror Film* (1992), horror critic Carol Clover insists that the anxieties surrounding gender differences distinguish themselves as a crucial theme in horror films.[3] Another critic, Natasha Patterson, furthers Clover's insistence on the importance of gender in horror, particularly the zombie film, even as she critiques her.[4] Still, both feminist critics are guilty of creating a framework that "privileges sexual difference [and] actively suppresses recognition of race, reenacting and mirroring the erasure of black womanhood that occurs in films, silencing any discussion of racial difference— of racialized sexual difference."[5] "Identificatory permeability" in regards to gender, specifically in the final girl or the rape-revenge protagonist, and the creation of a democratic textual viewing space with the female survivor of the zombie apocalypse unfortunately default to explorations of white womanhood. Brigid Cherry recognizes this folly and insists that "one factor of identity cannot easily be analyzed without considering others: gendered identities can be strongly linked to class or racial identity . . . and the one cannot be discussed without the other."[6] Clover's and Patterson's neglect of the powerful implications of the intersections of identity, particularly in regards to the constructions of black femininity, severely undercuts the strength of their theoretical approaches to how gender operates in horror.

The final girl is the protagonist of the slasher film who represents a surprising amalgam of differing normative gender constructions to connote an active defense of nimble strength and mental acuity. Clover depicts how the theory of the final girl proves to be an interesting taxonomy of specific character traits. The final girl "fight[s] back . . . with ferocity and even kill[s] the killer on [her] own, without help from the outside."[7] The final girl is intelligent and resourceful, particularly in the closing fight with the film's killer where she viciously battles for her life through a gauntlet testing both her mental and physical toughness. And it is the genre of horror that allows the final girl so much room for agency. Cherry deems the final girl fascinating because she subverts Western patriarchy on multiple levels. She confronts those societal forces that threaten women because there is no authority figure to intervene, and she must survive using her own capabilities.[8]

The most interesting characteristic of the final girl is that she is sexually unavailable, chiefly because she is not wholly feminine in her depiction; in fact, she is quite boyish in both construction and name: "Her smartness, gravity, competence in mechanical and other practical matters, and sexual reluctance set her apart from the other girls and ally her, ironically, with the very boys she fears or rejects, not to speak of the killer himself."[9] Clover's theory of the final girl relies upon the normativity of whiteness. This is evident in the theory's lack of sustainability when the raced intersection of blackness is laid upon it.

The admirable masculinization of Clover's final girl becomes incredibly problematic when she is racially read as black. Her blackness heightens her masculinity, demonstrating the "perceived inherent masculinity of blackness."[10] Calvin Hernton problematically notes that the historical enslavement of black women "has produced in many Negro females a sort of 'studism' which expressed itself in a strong matriarchal drive . . . black women are too demanding, too strict, too inconsiderate and too 'masculine.'"[11] Hortense Spillers criticizes the tendencies of twentieth-century scholars, both black and white, male and female, to pathologize black women for possessing survival skills developed in a racist, sexist, and classist world constructed against them: "the African-American female's 'dominance' and 'strength' come to be interpreted by later generations—both black and white, oddly enough—as a 'pathology,' as an instrument of castration."[12] The display of strength in unimaginable circumstances easily parallels the experiences of the final girl in the horror film's concluding chase scene. The coping mechanisms black women developed to deal with their multiple oppressions become a detriment to this particular characterization in contemporary horror. For the black woman's display of strength is read pejoratively even as the strength of the (white) final girl is read as positive, plucky instead of pathological, independent initiative and not a series of acts threatening castration.

The racial realities of the black woman shift the framework of Clover's criticism. The final girl is significant because of the white male audience member's ability to identify easily with her peril and fight for survival. I build upon what Clover refers to as the "majority viewer" of horror films—young males—which I expand to include their assumed whiteness, heterosexuality, and middle-classness. The crux of Clover's criticism pivots upon her insistence that the viewer's "identificatory powers are unbelievably elastic" particularly in regard to gender.[13] Yet I believe this insistence should be pushed further, for Clover fails to account for how or if the "majority viewer" can be as malleable with his identity in terms of race, particularly at the same time as he is being so elastic in terms of gender.

The problematic assumption of whiteness as a foundation for Clover's theoretical outline reemerges with the rape-revenge protagonist. This particular horror plot centers on the appalling physical and mental violation of a (usually) female protagonist by one or more male individuals. The ghastliness of the plot continues with the central character's terrifically violent revenge visited upon her perpetrators as a vengeful vigilante. Its success hinges upon the male viewer's ability to identify with the gruesome trauma visited upon and conducted by the central female character. Clover insists that the act of rape in these films is far larger than an individual violation of the protagonist but also serves as a "social and political act . . . [that comments upon] the power dynamic between men and women that makes rape happen in the first place and . . . that makes it so eminently avengeable."[14] The rape-revenge protagonist lays bare the pervasiveness of the structural misogyny that permeates Western society and how women live in constant threat of its consuming powers.[15] Clover's findings are incredibly significant for their ability to allow horror's majority viewer to identify with the problems that occur with gender difference, such as the complex identificatory slippage that occurs with experiencing the rape and victimization of an (often) female protagonist. Yet again, acknowledging the layer of race allows for a more holistic view of the societal structures that oppress all women, not just white women.

Natasha Patterson's "Cannibalizing Gender and Genre: A Feminist Re-Vision of George Romero's Zombie Films" focuses specifically upon zombie horror. Patterson believes that zombie narratives "make possible alternative visions of femininity, opening up spaces for the female viewer that do not rely significantly on gender stereotypes that anticipate the passivity or masochism of the female viewer."[16] Here, Patterson uses Romero to expose yet another weakness in Clover's theory of "identificatory permeability," for it assumes that the viewer can easily identify the lines between gender identity and the oscillation that occurs between them.[17] Patterson insists that "Romero's films refute any notion of a 'gendered gaze'" and expands her analysis beyond the "majority viewer" to include the experiences of female observers.[18] Patterson thereby proposes the concept of a "democratic textual viewing space," which is "[a] state of spectatorial ambivalence . . . due to my simultaneous feelings of fear and fascination . . . in which I am able to question things, even as I recognize my own complicity with social inequalities."[19] I choose to push Patterson's concept of democratic textual viewing space further, beyond her feminist inclusion of a normatively white female gaze with which to examine the all-assuming whiteness of the zombie text. Patterson's democracy remains exclusive to the tenets of whiteness: "it does not even consider the possibility that women can construct an oppositional gaze via an understanding and awareness of the politics of race and racism."[20] Contemporary horror theory must surpass the exclusivity of the idea that all womanhood is white; this chapter demands that critical examinations of blackness and womanhood must ensue.

All the Blacks Are Men

Contemporary feminist criticism has built paradigms such as the final girl and the rape-revenge protagonist over the last thirty years with which to evaluate how gender is characterized in postmodern horror fiction.[21] Unfortunately, much of horror criticism—including feminist horror criticism—has been limited to the construction of women in horror films, which typically feature lithe and attractive women being violently dismembered by psychotic killers. Concurrently, critics who study race theory have continued to analyze how people of color (specifically blacks) have been filmically depicted as monstrous.[22] However, much of this study has been relegated to the realm of blaxploitation films, particularly the construction of male characters in that genre. There remains a marked dearth of criticism on the portrayal of black women within the genre of horror, even as horror has reemerged as a pop culture and academic phenomenon.

Scholars such as Aalya Ahmad, Harry M. Benshoff, Robin R. Means-Coleman, Annalee Newitz, Isabel Piñedo, and Robin Wood have examined blackness in horror, but their studies of it—even those feminist studies among them—have mostly centered on the textual experiences of black men, with some minimal attention paid to black men as viewers.[23] This reality highlights that black women are again made invisible when horror criticism discusses race. Thus, in this chapter I investigate how two critics examine the intersections of blackness and monstrosity in order to highlight the blind spots of contemporary criticism. Cultural critic Annalee Newitz explores how the monstrosities of black bodies and white anxiety comment upon the instability of Western capitalism, while film critic Harry M. Benshoff examines the black gaze and reimagines the queering of blaxploitation cinema. Benshoff, whose analysis proves quite encompassing, even attempts to outline an approach to black women in blaxploitation horror, although the majority of his treatment centers on black men. Still, throughout the growing amount of critical work done on blacks in horror, these "interrogating black looks [are] mainly concerned with issues of race and racism, the way racial domination of blacks by whites overdetermine[s] representation. They [are] rarely concerned with gender."[24] It is here that I appreciate the foundations that have been laid, but my contention is that none of the aforementioned horror frameworks address the peculiarities of black women's positionality. My intervention uses a black feminist framework to engage in nascent horror theories that articulate and establish a critical space for black women.

The following critical race analyses of horror texts reveal the urgent need for my racially gendered critique. In *Pretend We're Dead: Capitalist Monsters in American Pop Culture*, Annalee Newitz's examination of the undead in horror texts acknowledges the dread of racial difference that so often permeates the works, yet still manages to center itself on an (albeit incredibly interesting) examination of whiteness. Newitz insists that zombie films of both the past and present explore the dis-ease and growing horror at the increasing instability of white supremacy, and that the reality of zombies represents the "demise of white power and Western rationalism."[25] Newitz reads George Romero's *Night of the Living Dead* as just as much a treatise on class as on race, particularly in her analysis of the central character, Ben. Ben is an educated leader, and his raced blackness is aptly juxtaposed against the overwhelming horror of the raced whiteness of the swarms of zombies that plague the living. Ben appears lively and dynamic when read against the catatonic Barbra and the shuffling zombies. Ben is a "*middle-class* black hero" who is ultimately destroyed by a "self-defeating, dying whiteness" as he is killed not by a zombie, but by a mob of white men with guns who mistake him for a zombie.[26] Newitz implicitly suggests that this mistaken identity is purposeful, that the mob is unable and unwilling to distinguish the differences between a black male who is a monstrous zombie and a black male survivor. He dies simply because he is a black man with power in a white-dominated world.

A similar end finds African Prince Mumawaldee, best known as the titular lead of *Blacula* (1972), who is critiqued by Benshoff along with other blaxploitation horror monsters in his essay "Blaxploitation Horror Films: Generic Reappropriation or Reinscription?" as "agents of black pride and black power" for they "depicted a stronger, more militant image of African Americans who triumphed over white antagonists."[27] This sympathetic reimagining of Blacula and other black monsters like him reveals the negotiated gaze of the marginalized black community. These audience members "identify with monsters out to topple dominant social institutions (that oppress both movie monsters and real-life minorities) in ways that can be a pleasurable and potentially empowering act for many film goers."[28] Instead of seeing him as a perpetrator of vampiric evil upon the black community, Benshoff suggests that Blacula is an incredibly sympathetic character whose curse of vampirism becomes a metaphor for the "lingering legacy of racism" that "enslaved" him.[29] Blacula also revises W.E.B. Du Bois's theory of double-consciousness, for he must struggle between his two identities as a deposed African prince and a European vampire.[30] Though powerful, critiques of black horror must continue moving beyond a centering on the black male experience to the oppositional gaze. Racism is continuously gendered, even in these readings of Ben and Blacula; their masculinity is a threat to white patriarchal power that must be destroyed. How can critics continue to focus their theories on less than half of the black population?

Benshoff attempts to incorporate a reading of black women in horror, though his analysis is hindered by the limited textual data the blaxploitation horror film genre provides. While these films often prove successful in their critique of race, "[they] were unable to withstand the genre's more regular demonization of gender and sexuality, which are arguably more deeply embedded as monstrous within both the horror film and the culture at large."[31] Blaxploitation horror films such as *Abby* (1974) and *Sugar Hill* (1974) featured black women as lead characters, yet remained incredibly problematic. Benshoff successfully critiques the genre for upholding an antiquated ideal of black machismo, often at the cost of complex female characters along with the development of the blaxploitation superwoman, whose abnormal strength threatens the masculinity of the central male protagonist.

I contend that the monstrosity of black women stems from this stereotype of the black Superwoman, also known as the "strong black woman." Michele Wallace describes it as "[an] intricate web of mythology surround[ing] the black woman, [in which] a fundamental image emerges . . . she is a Superwoman."[32] This mythology includes the "problematic assumptions" that "strong Black women are the stark and deviant opposites of weak and appropriately feminine white women, that strength is a natural quality of Black women and a litmus test for their womanhood, and that being strong accurately characterizes Black women's motivations and behaviors."[33] This trope actively dehumanizes black women, contributing to their Otherness and hindering the identificatory permeability that allows audience members to identify with black male monsters. The characterization of the black woman as overly strong and superhuman in all aspects is a method of dehumanization.[34] Zora Neale Hurston famously spoke to this active dehumanization in *Their Eyes Were Watching God* when Nanny states that "de nigger woman is de mule uh de world."[35] Constructions of black women as unnaturally strong and the pernicious effect of this have been examined in multiple areas of black feminist studies. Trudier Harris pathologizes this so-called strength as a disease, termed the "virus of strength," a "form of ill health [that] perpetuates dysfunction in literary families."[36] Sociologist Patricia Hill Collins deems the strong black woman one of the "controlling images" that prevents black women from achieving self-actualization both within and outside of the black community. Concurrently, Tamara Beauboeuf-Lafontant insists that the strong black woman presents a "problematic discourse" where "strength is likened to a performance and a façade rather than an honest reflection of Black women" that privileges self-silencing and self-negation.[37] The most dangerous aspect of the "strong black woman" is her inherent simplicity. Such a stigmatype ignores the complexity of black womanhood and its radical potential to subvert multiple problematic identities simultaneously.

Thus, the very presence of black women in the horror text complicates existing horror theory on black monstrosity. Black female monsters have a history that begins in slavery, much like *Blacula*'s Prince Mumuwalde. However, although they are women, they were whipped and lynched without equivocation, and their sex was rarely, if ever, a mitigating circumstance in the meting out of punishment. Sugar, the black female protagonist, uses Vodou gods (loas) and rituals to raise zombies who were former slaves to avenge her fiancé's murder. Her hair becomes a natural Afro, a far more Africanized style whenever she employs the zombies.[38] But she also explicitly and continuously runs into racialized sexism in her quest for vengeance. She is unable to rely upon sheer force to entrap these men; the movie implies that she outsources her violence using voodoo because she is a woman. As the men are lured to their deaths, Sugar is shown using her "feminine wiles." The men repeatedly characterize and denigrate her very existence as a black woman, particularly in regards to the voracious sexual appetites associated with black women.[39] In the end, Sugar exacts her revenge, but only by reinforcing dangerous sexual stereotypes of black women. Thus, Sugar's potential as a subversive character is heavily muted by blaxploitation gender dynamics.

The pernicious falsehoods that are associated with black female sexuality also contribute to their Otherness as black female monsters. The construction of black women's sexuality in the Western hegemonic imaginary has, more often than not, been defined against the sexual mores constructed for white women. Many of these mores were established during slavery and became more explicitly defined in the nineteenth-century's Cult of True Womanhood. The ideology of True Womanhood identified four cardinal virtues of white womanhood: piety, purity, submissiveness, and domesticity.[40] True women had "delicate constitutions" and were "easily fatigued."[41] Hazel V. Carby notes that these values were the opposite qualifications of what was required to survive as a black woman in the century; "an absence of the qualities of piety and purity [was] a crucial signifier."[42] Black women were actively excluded from what became the functioning definition of womanhood. Carby insists that "white women were constructed as chaste even as black women were portrayed as overtly sexual."[43] Notably, it is this context that produced the stereotype of the black Jezebel, the sexually avaricious black girl/woman who seduces the white male slave master/overseer. Thus, black women continue the cultural tradition of Sycorax, a characterization to be defined against, marginalized, and passive in actualization. Yet by dismantling the hierarchies of the hegemony, black feminist cultural critics discover the radical possibilities of black woman–centered critiques.

bell hooks finds power in the act of "looking back" directly into the face of hegemonic power.[44] She hearkens back to its subversive power and trauma among African Americans. The black enslaved are punished for looking inappropriately at white authority figures; Jim Crow America brutally murders the young Emmitt Till for looking at a white woman.[45] Even today, young black men are tasered, beaten, and killed by police officers for the subversive act of "eye-fucking."[46] hooks refers to the gaze as an act in which powerful subversion intertwines with trauma. Looking back is a dangerous temptation that must be used wisely, for if noticed by the receiver of this gaze, consequences may range from reprimand to death.

Hegemonic power as domination controls the power of the gaze, yet the act of watching film has the potential for power.[47] Its privilege is demonstrated in the inability of the marginalized to openly possess it. But film is watched in the darkness of a movie theater, the privacy of one's home, and in the public privacy of the coffee shop listening to headphones. The dominant's display of the spectacle of film lays itself bare and makes it vulnerable to those it actively ignores and casts out. It is here that a slippage occurs and oppositional readings formulate and ferment, for the act of viewership by the marginalized becomes an individuated experience outside of the dominant's purview. In these ruptures that the hegemony fails to recognize, the very act of looking has become "a site of resistance."[48]

hooks recognizes the potential of the filmic as an opportunity for black women to employ what she terms the oppositional gaze by building upon the hesitancy among this critical population because of film's historic erasure of black women.[49] Black women have always had a negotiated reading of film. It is a necessary act to ensure their psychic survival in a genre that has limited the potentiality of their lived realities to mammies, Sapphires, and Jezebels, and only when it has chosen to acknowledge their existence at all. Black women watch films wholly acknowledging that those images are part of "a system of knowledge and power reproducing and maintaining white supremacy."[50] These women approach a complicated space of agency where they "experience viewing pleasure in a context where looking was also about contestation and confrontation." hooks takes what had so often been thought of as a subjugated position of black women for their "absent presence" in cinema studies and revises it, privileging their act of looking as one that is exclusive and gained only through years of lived experiences outside the powerfully complicated constructions of race and patriarchy that inform the foundations of film theory. For black women actively refuse to identify with either the victim of the gaze or its perpetrator, excavating a place of agency (rupture/disjuncture) outside of the powerful dynamic.

The oppositional gaze is named as the result of the "resistance, struggle, reading, and looking 'against the grain,' that black women have been able to value our process of looking."[51] hooks advocates for black women to "star[e] dangerously," embodying a specific sense of knowing and critique that uniquely enhances both feminist film studies and critical race theory.[52] Still it must be acknowledged that the viewing pleasure that black women could experience was often heavily mediated by their peculiar position—a mediation that often turned to pain.[53] And again hooks revises, by constructing the oppositional gaze as "a theory of looking relations where the cinematic visual delight is the pleasure of *interrogation*."[54] Following the critical backlash against the tiresome characterizations of white manhood, *Searching for Sycorax* demands an increase in the number of contemporary horror texts that feature and center significant and complicated characterizations of black women.[55]

Centering the white male experience and its repugnant fascination with black men or white women is not only problematic, it ultimately fails to illustrate the various intersections of race and gender that interrogate whiteness and maleness. Furthermore, this practice remains incredibly exclusionary, propagating the Western hierarchical framework of privileging the experiences of the white male. I contend that critically exploring, via an oppositional gaze, the characterizations of black females, both monstrous and non-monstrous, pushes horror theory to mine the critically rich ores of the intersections of race and gender.

"The female look—a look given preeminent position in the horror film—shares the male fear of the monster's freakishness, but also recognizes the sense in which this freakishness is similar to her own difference."[56] Brigid Cherry acknowledges that the identities of audiences heavily affect their negotiated viewing of the film text, and Benshoff names this effect an act of "queering" the text.[57] I push these critical ideas further by integrating them together, informing the oppositional gaze as an act of viewing the horror text from a place of rupture—the marginalized position of black women—which influences their negotiated reading of a text that either ignores them or deems them freakish monstrosities. Black women are so far removed from the "majority viewer" that they can find powerful subversive potential in the disjunctures of zombie horror texts.[58] The oppositional gaze moves beyond the democratic textual viewing space in which Patterson advocates, for its grounding in whiteness prevents a true democracy. Black women are critical spectators from a location that is disrupted. It is from this rupture, this interstice outside the mainstream, that I have critiqued the gaps found in previous horror theory, and it is also from this rupture that I will analyze contemporary zombie texts of Robert Kirkland and Danny Boyle. I advocate for all horror critics—not simply black women—to use and expand the oppositional gaze, to move beyond the simple binaries that too many Western horror texts perpetuate. Horror critics must move beyond identificatory permeability to a sustained interrogation of the assumed majority status, of male and female, black and white, and the oscillations in-between, as well as any other intersectional identifications of the viewer.

Black Women as Complicated Characters of Zombie Horror

George Romero centers his classic movies on the zombies themselves: he appears cinematically obsessed with how well zombies display a humanity that is often more powerful than that of the humans themselves. Natasha Patterson believes that Romero is calling for societal destabilization by continually drawing the viewer's gaze to the zombie and away from the humans.[59] Newer creators in the genre shift the focus to the mental and physical states of the survivors. After the initial onslaught of blood, horror, and guts, the zombies become a background of groans, an ever-present danger to the text's characters, an important cause for concern, but rarely the main focus of the ongoing psychological drama.[60] The difference is crucial because the focus upon the survivors offers a glimpse into the potential to actively revise societal hierarchies as a matter of survival. The decisions, discussions, and emergence of leaders attempt to subvert our traditional cultural hegemonies, but far too often the tensions explored and their resulting consequences simply reinforce them.

Danny Boyle's *28 Days Later* (2002) and Robert Kirkman's *The Walking Dead* (2003) both contain complex constructions of black female characters, Selena and Michonne, respectively. These characters, though groundbreaking by virtue of their very presence, still necessitate a critique of their construction from the analytical ruptures of black feminist theory. They must be examined within their sociocritical contexts and from the standpoint of how they reimagine classically gendered horror movie constructions. Both authors also place classic horror film tropes pertaining to women within a zombie context. Kirkman racializes the rape-revenge protagonist in his creation of Michonne, while Boyle uses Selena as a fresh take on the final girl. Each creator uses the dynamics of zombie horror film to broach the stereotypes that riddle the constructions of the strong black woman, the stereotypes of black female sexuality, and the powerful race and gender dynamics that influence the systematic rape of black women.[61] Finally, I posit that Boyle is successful in complicating Selena even as Kirkman's attempt to bring complexity to his characterization of Michonne ultimately fails in his surrender of deepening her characterization to privileging the revelation of another facet of The Governor.[62]

Michonne and Selena complicate their respective horror film female protagonistic tropes in their constructions as the stereotypical "strong black woman." It is necessary to note that the perpetuation of the "strong black woman'" stereotype expands beyond the limited scope of black female monsters and becomes insidiously applicable to black female characterizations in horror texts as a whole, and zombie texts in particular. Too often, the supposed inordinate strength of black women becomes the starting point for all characterizations of black women, be they monstrous or not. I insist that this textual reality interferes with the identificatory permeability majority viewers are able to experience with (white) female protagonists. The dehumanization that occurs with this stereotype, even as it occurs to a lesser extent than with black female monsters, is a hurdle that must be acknowledged and overcome within contemporary zombie theory. Kirkman and Boyle successfully initiate a subversion of the stereotype by building upon it, expanding its parameters as they begin to construct multifaceted black women characters who are allowed to possess the full range of their humanity.[63] Yet mainstream contemporary horror criticism has yet to catch up to the transgressive nature of characters such as Michonne and Selena, and this is why this project's intervention proves necessary.

Michonne is shown as a strong black woman from the moment she is introduced with a stoic silence. She arrives at the prison that Rick Grimes and the other survivors have taken over dressed in a hooded cape and accompanied by two coffled, rotted zombies who follow her lead obediently. Michonne enters the prison compound after proving her worthiness and saving the life of one of the survivors. Her construction as the strong black woman continues as she settles into life in the compound. She has quickly adapted to the new dangers of a world occupied by zombies, an adaptability Kirkman has heretofore associated only with his male characters. For "the construction of strength [among black women] allows both onlookers and a woman herself to de-emphasize her struggle, to disconnect from any assistance, and to turn a blind eye to the real oppression in the context she is facing."[64] Michonne is differentiated as her story slowly unfolds to the readers. She no longer defines herself as a mother: "I had two kids. Two girls. I also had a boyfriend, a mother, a brother, two sisters, an ex-husband, a job, a mortgage, and a whole lot of other stuff. I don't have a whole hell of a lot anymore. Things have changed."[65] These horrific losses are similar to those recounted and experienced by so many other characters in the comic, but none has carried their burden with the quiet endurance of Michonne, the embodiment of the strong black woman.

Michonne's creation as a black woman not only distinguishes the raced and gendered Otherness of her character, it allows each construction to build upon and compound the impact of the other. Kirkman continues to highlight Michonne's difference as she is also shown making expert use of a katana to dispatch a bothersome zombie.[66] Her blackness is implicitly associated with a certain masculinity that actively separates her from the rote ideas of femininity associated with the ideals of white womanhood: demure, domestic, delicate, and in constant need of male protection. Michonne possesses a sense of capability heretofore unseen in any of the (white) women in the series who have been purposely domesticated and typically feminized.[67] No other women in the group possess such a capability to protect themselves in such dangerous circumstances. Rick teaches his seven-year-old son, Carl, how to shoot properly, yet fails to do the same for his adult wife, Lori. The women are routinely sent away to complete such domestic duties as laundry and child care while the men forage for food and fight zombies. Only Andrea, a young white woman, becomes quite adept as a markswoman, particularly with a rifle. Yet her capabilities with the rifle are tempered by her de facto adoption of Mitch and Donna's twins. Her femininity is again solidified by her marked talent as a seamstress for the entire group.[68]

Kirkman begins constructing Michonne as a racially gendered stereotype, but then he begins to complicate her characterization by allowing her to explicitly express vulnerability. After spending some time in the compound, the panels show a close-up of her face as she is having an earnest conversation with someone, attempting to convince the other person that she has made the right decision in coming to the prison for safety. The conversation is interrupted by another character, and the panel then expands to a wide shot that takes up the entire page, showing an empty room.[69] This exchange demonstrates that Michonne is not inscrutable. She needs someone to talk to; she needs help to survive like any other character; she has simply been alone so long that she has developed dissociative personalities to cope with the tragedy associated with the zombie apocalypse.

Michonne continues to complicate the stereotype of the strong black woman by establishing a connection to the other black male character, Tyrese, whom she befriends and eventually seduces. She and Tyrese find a kindredness in spirit as they converse and find multiple areas of mutual interests. Different facets of Michonne begin to emerge, illuminating a dawning complexity—we learn that she is a former athlete, enjoyed watching and playing sports, and loves to workout and lift weights. Still, Michonne's seduction of Tyrese proves problematic, for it is presented in direct contrast against the construction of Tyrese's blond-haired, light-eyed girl-friend, Carol, who is presented as typically "feminine" and contin-ually needs male protection. Tyrese is portrayed as being actively seduced by Michonne, who clearly knows of his relationship with Carol. His words and his own personal agency are overshadowed by the unstoppable sexuality of Michonne, for the black Superwoman is infinite in her sexual appetites.[70] The nature of the sex between Michonne and Tyrese and its presentation are also illicit. There is no romance, no tender acts are portrayed; Michonne barely even speaks. She simply performs fellatio upon Tyrese despite his (weak) protest. This scene is significant particularly when it is placed within the historic context of black women's sexuality. Frances Smith Foster insists that "black women became closely identified with illicit sex. . . . She was not pure and thus not a model of womanhood."[71] Kirkman clearly juxtaposes Michonne's willing-ness to perform "dirty" sexual acts against Carol's reaction to oral sex. Carol is portrayed as beyond unwilling; she is literally unable to perform the act, evidence of her conjugal sanctity.[72] Again, the issue of normativity arises. Michonne performs a non-procreative and therefore non-normative act upon Tyrese, further distinguish-ing her sexuality from that of Carol.

Kirkman also uses the placement of Michonne in a zombie context to reimagine the parameters of the rape-revenge protagonist. The rape of black women is an American institution fraught with intertwined histories of race, gender, and class. Feminist critic Dorri R. Beam insists that our patriarchal society has consistently refused to view rape as a hate crime.[73] The work of Carla Peterson demonstrates that rape has been viewed as an act of passion (consensual or not) in which the woman is somehow complicit.[74] Peterson ultimately suggests that the reality of black women's status as unfeminine and not worthy of protection renders them vulnerable and more isolated in our patriarchal society.[75] This reality coalesces with Clover's assessment of women under the constant threat of sexual and psychological violence. Still, I suggest that the lack of whiteness, and the protection and sympathy that whiteness imparts, heightens the bodily threat to black women. Hazel Carby denigrates the fact that "the institutionalized rape of black women has never been as powerful a symbol of black oppression as the spectacle of lynching."[76] Further, I insist that the women's raced blackness dampens, to stay within Clover's lexicon, the majority's viewer's "identificatory permeability" with a black female rape-revenge protagonist.

Michonne embodies the classic paradigm of the rape-revenge protagonist, for she is brutally gang raped and enacts a horrifically violent revenge upon her lead perpetrator, The Governor.[77] Her attack reveals the omnipresent nature of misogyny in Western culture, but the construction of Michonne as a black woman also exposes the reader to the insidious nature of racism in contemporary Western society. The masculinity associated with her raced blackness illustrates that her womanhood is not the only qualifier in her subjugation. Michonne is raped to emphasize her femininity and, later, placed in a gladiator ring replete with zombies highlighting her masculinity as a fighter.[78] Michonne's intersecting identities demand more from Clover's rape-revenge protagonist paradigm, for her intersections necessitate an expansion that includes race.

Michonne's character introduction demonstrates the dangers of incorporating black women characters while failing to truly

FIG. 4. Michonne in *The Walking Dead* issue 29, by Robert Kirkman and Charlie Adlard (2006).

bring their complexity to the fore. Kirkman hints at the existence of multiple facets of her character, yet chooses to sacrifice her individuation to the demands of the narrative. Michonne's racially gendered construction marks her as rapeable, as a character whose complex potentiality is forfeited. Michonne allows Kirkman to horrify his readers without alienating them—something that could not have occurred with any of Kirkman's other (white) female characters. Kirkman lazily relies on the creative myth of the strong black woman to show that Michonne is "a machine" for whom sympathy and complexity need not exist.[79] Concurrently, Danny Boyle grounds his characterization of Selena in stereotypes long enough to shatter them with the development of multiple facets of her character's ideation.

Boyle's early establishment of Selena's characterization moors itself in her toughness as "a strong black woman." She is adamant in her willingness to kill anything that threatens her life in a world filled with the infected. She proves this tenacity in both word and deed, explicitly explaining the rules she lives by to Jim, including her willingness to kill him "in a heartbeat" if he becomes infected. But Selena is simply reiterating a visually established fact, for she has already murdered fellow survivor Mark, immediately and without compunction once she discerns he has been infected. Selena's emotional and physical toughness is highlighted by the continuous presence of her machete. Selena's machete also racializes her. The machete is not only phallic, it is a specific tool associated with people of the tropics, people of color, and, in Britain, Africans from the nation's colonized diaspora.

Selena's tough attitude and ever-present machete are not the only characteristics that mark her as the "strong black woman": Jim's (and the audience's) expectations of her as a maternal figure tap into the quintessential mothering often associated with black women. Boyle deliberately constructs the initial relationship between Jim and Selena as similar to that between a mother and child. Selena steadily admonishes him for his curiosity in such a dangerous environment, whether it is for his entering unknown buildings without caution or not taking proper care of himself in their dire circumstances. Jim is an active participant in the maternal nature of their relationship; it is Selena's name he screams for help each time he is in danger. He even comments after she warns him not to go into a building, "It's like going on holiday with my bloody Aunt."

Still, the masculinity associated with the strong black woman allows Selena to easily embody Clover's paradigm of the final girl. In complete contrast to Michonne's Othered introduction, the only thing highlighted by Selena's introduction is her humanity. Selena and Mark are introduced, saving an imperiled Jim from a group of the infected. This movie scene is typified by a frenzied action and a violent end to the infected as they are burned by the purposeful explosion of a gas station. Selena runs into the frame

FIG. 5. Naomie Harris as Selena, *28 Days Later* (2002).

completely covered in clothing as protection from the infected's bodily fluids. Her hair is covered, she wears glasses, and her face is enclosed in a scarf to protect her mouth. The rest of her body is covered in normative everyday Western wear—jeans, a top, sensible shoes, and a leather trench. This introduction not only makes plot sense, it also shows Boyle's willingness to subvert the Western propensity to place characters within easily defined boxes. Mark is just as protectively covered, and the only thing we, the audience, can infer from the two characters is that they are human, capable, and not infected. Selena is only gendered later, through her voice, as she advises Jim to protect himself from the coming explosion.

Boyle also constructs Selena as relatively chaste in nature. Once Jim and Selena meet the father-daughter unit of Frank and Hannah, their friendship is given time to develop in the safety of the family's home. Selena is allowed to be innocent and sweet, to participate in the slow building of an equal relationship with Jim. Selena's sexuality is multifaceted. She no longer acts like Jim's mother, and he no longer cries out for her to save him, for he becomes just as self-sufficient as she. Their unusual courtship moves forward with a chaste kiss wholly different from the overt sexuality of Michonne. Selena is allowed the combination of sexual freedom (it is she who initiates the kiss) and the chastity usually associated with the constructed sexuality of white women (she apologizes for her forwardness). These changes develop organically and continue to grow.

Yet Selena complicates Clover's paradigm of the final girl not simply because of her race but also by being placed within a zombie context. She displays inordinate amounts of mental and physical toughness, but the final fight is not hers alone. Selena does not fight against the danger of one slasher (for example, Michael Myers), but the threat of multiple human survivors *and* the infected. She must employ the strength of the communal bonds she has established with her new "family" to survive intact; there is no room for individuality. Selena and Hannah use their quick wits to defend against their attempted rapes by the unit of soldiers they thought would provide protection. Although she has previously shown the chaste nature of her sexuality with Jim in previous scenes, her race contributes to the soldiers' sexual desire for her as one of them proclaims while the others shake their head in agreement: "I want the black one!"

Selena does not allow this racialized sexism deter her from survival, displaying an enduring stubbornness to live that characterizes the final girl. She initiates affection with one soldier in order to buy time for her to create a better plan to ensure the safety of both herself and the young Hannah. In this situation Selena shows a multifaceted level of intelligence and resourcefulness that moves her beyond the broad strokes of stereotypes and allows her to embody the trope of the final girl. Her strength is shown as she outwits the soldiers, cares for Hannah, and stalls for time to figure out what to do. Selena's agency as the final girl is aided by the external actions of Jim as he distracts the soldiers from their licentious intentions. It is reestablished that Selena can protect herself, but she is also shown being protected by Jim and working together with Hannah to survive a mansion full of rapacious soldiers and manic infected. Her working partnerships with her newly found family ensure her eventual survival and allow her a safe space to grow beyond a willingness to kill Jim "in a heartbeat."

The inclusion of multifaceted black women characters such as Michonne and Selena in horror texts not only expands the audience, it increases the potentiality of the horror genre itself. Their very existence strengthens contemporary zombie and horror theory by complicating the theory and making it flexible enough to encompass and demonstrate the multiple intersections of identity even as it broadens the audiences of the genre, ensuring its survival and relevance. It is not enough to simply include black female characters, but creators must also make them individuated figures woven within the major narrative. I insist that the demonstrated dangers of normativity in horror must be challenged by interrogating the theory with the plethora of racially gendered intersections that exist within and without the Western hegemony. Furthermore, these practices can only be continually subverted by others creating texts that are outside of hegemonies of Hollywood and/or major comic book publishers.[80] The following chapters demonstrate the potentiality of black women creators who produce texts that subvert the flawed construction of the majority viewer and create projects that revise horror on their terms. Contemporary black women genre writers are talking back to the hegemony by defining themselves by revising horror studies.

2

Black Feminism and the Struggle for Literary Respectability

What I want to advocate is that black feminist criticism be regarded
critically as a problem, not a solution, as a sign
that should be interrogated, a locus of contradictions.
—Hazel V. Carby

It is the idea that speculative fiction is somehow an indulgence or that it
is trivial that seems the most probable reason for its dismissal by literary
critics as well as its lack of appeal to most Black readers or authors.
—Jewelle Gomez

To whom are we accountable? And what social relations are in/scribing us?
—Barbara Christian

The search for Sycorax does not develop from a vacuum of black
feminism, nor can its subversive nature only be ascribed as a healing
salve for the racially gendered wounds inflicted by horror studies.
In the previous chapter, I discussed how horror criticism has failed
in articulating a complex space for black women as well as the
problematic nature of condemning black women's characterizations to manifestations of monstrosity. In this chapter, I turn
my critique to how black feminist literary theory lacks a space for

horror and how it proves detrimental in the recognition of the complexities of black women creators.[1] In truth, the investigation of black women and horror is not a new concept in literature—critics such as Sandra Jackson, Susana Morris, and Gina Wisker have conducted strong black feminist readings of various horror writers and films.[2] Robin Means Coleman's *Horror Noire: Black in American Horror Films from the 1890s to Present* (2011) devotes a significant portion of its critique to the study of black women character constructions in film through a black feminist lens. Yet in this chapter, I choose to focus my investigation on examining the whys of horror criticism's failure to establish a significant and sustained space within black feminist literary frameworks. I interrogate black feminist literary theory and its previous inability to create and support a sustained place for critical horror inquiry. I contend that the critical study of black women and horror has been routinely hindered by the politics of literary respectability that defined black feminist literary theory in the final thirty years of the twentieth century as it struggled to be accepted into the academy.

This chapter has three interconnected sections that build upon the central task of establishing a historical context and argument for the study of black women writing horror. I begin by quickly defining black feminist literary theory by demonstrating its nascence as an epistemological framework that informs critical readings of texts and establishes a black women's literary tradition. Next, I argue that black feminist literary theory—often assumed to be revolutionary in its purposes—has proven surprisingly conservative as its creators engaged in a fight for literary respectability in academia. I end this chapter by reiterating horror criticism not only as a valid critical framework but also as an episteme that illuminates new and fertile paths for reading black women's texts.

Black Feminist Theory

Black feminist theory began in the nineteenth century, developing as a part of the abolitionist and suffragette movements and

FIG. 6. Clockwise from top left: Fanny Jackson Coppin, Frances Ellen Watkins Harper, Ida Bell Wells, Anna J. Cooper, and Octavia Butler.

flourishing during Reconstruction. Activists such as Frances E. W. Harper, Anna Julia Cooper, Ida B. Wells, and Fannie Jackson Coppin chiseled a space for black women and demanded recognition, inclusion, and authority in the aforementioned sociopolitical movements of American history. The women continuously found themselves facing a wall of indifference. It was difficult to convince others that the liberation of black womanhood would lead to the liberation of all women. Hazel V. Carby notes that "the struggle of black women to achieve adequate representation within the women's suffrage and temperance movements had been continually undermined by a pernicious and persistent racism."[3] A consistent lack of "fit" with the white suffrage movement, as well as a similar circumstance in the ongoing male-centered battle for the improvement of the Negro race revealed to black women the need to self-articulate a space that addressed the peculiar needs of black women.

For over a century, these women hewed spaces in which they flourished—through tenacious acts of working within the interstices of cultural production—in which black women's lived realities were theoretically interpreted by those who actually lived them.[4] The rich advancement of black feminist theory thrived in the final third of the twentieth century—the late 1960s through the early 1990s—it is this era that most piques my critical interest for this chapter's study.[5] This era was a renaissance for black women, amplifying critical and textual developments, offering multiple iterations of black feminisms across multiple disciplines and class identities, and among multiple racial and/or gendered communities. Most interesting, particularly for my critical interests, this epoch became heavily defined by the foothold black feminism gained in the academic establishment and the (problematic) hegemonic structures of the intelligentsia in which it came to actively participate.[6]

Black feminist theory is a "cultural-political" value system that articulates and creates "opportunities for Black women to carry out autonomously defined investigation of self in a society which—through racial, sexual, and class oppression—systematically denies that our existence has been, by definition, limited."[7] Critic Deborah McDowell insists that black women operate under a "simultaneity of oppressions" defined by their race, gender, and class status; black lesbians such as Barbara Smith also came to identify sexual, particularly queer, identities as an equitable system of oppression.[8] The unique positionality of black women—afforded by the multiple facets of their identities operating together—heavily influences their lived realities and subsequently infiltrates their social, political, and cultural output. The multiplicity that defines black women has also led to present fissures of incongruity that are not necessarily negative. Disagreements and tensions remain necessary demonstrations of growth, as they highlight that black women are not monolithic in their lived experiences and certainly not homogeneous in their theoretical extrapolations of those proficiencies. Even in the midst of disagreement, I use the next section to highlight that a situational consensus eventually began to develop on who would be considered the leading black feminist critics in literature as well as what were the most "appropriate" literary manifestations of black feminism and—most especially—who was writing it and who was not. It was this tenuous power structure, defined by black feminisms' own intelligentsia, that would consistently eschew black women's speculative literature in a misguided fight for literary respectability.

To Become a Respectable Black Woman

I would like to take a note from Hazel V. Carby and interrogate black feminist theory in and of itself.[9] This chapter is meant to act as a revelation, an evaluation of specific choices made by black feminist theory's literary leaders and their harmful effects upon those texts that did not easily fit into the movement's rigid goals of highlighting "appropriate" black feminist literature. Here, I establish a contention that I expound upon in subsequent chapters—I argue that contemporary black women horror writers are not ahistorical; they exist within the literary tradition black feminist criticism establishes and actively demonstrate their agility with prominent themes of black feminist literary theory.

Black feminist literary theory has claimed to act as a sustained critical project of subverting the Western literary hegemon—more specifically, the Canon. The Canon Wars of the latter third of the twentieth century sparked a movement for academic legitimacy among many black feminist literary theorists. Other critics believe that this fight for Canon acceptance was antithetical to black feminist literary theory as a whole. At times, these antithetical beliefs about the Canon sometimes existed within the same scholar.[10] Subversive projects within the Western hegemony requires the consolidation of capital both within and outside of its institution, and I contend that early black feminist literary critics participated in a concerted effort to include black women's writings declared as worthy of being titled *literature*.[11] I insist that there was a successful privileging of specific authors and readings of their works, such as Toni Morrison, Alice Walker, Gloria Naylor, Ann Petry, Zora Neale Hurston, and others. This section's intervention also centers on a harsh reality—that other writers and readings of the aforementioned authors' works that were associated with "lower" subgenres such as horror, science fiction, and fantasy were actively ignored, passively neglected, and/or marginalized to spaces in which they were not sufficiently nurtured.

The overarching questions of this section remain who made these choices and what were the specific parameters of determining whose writing was worthy of highlighting and pushed as exemplars of black women's literature? To properly answer these questions, I find it necessary to return to an early incarnation of black feminist theory—the social movement of black women's respectability politics in the late nineteenth and early twentieth centuries. Respectability politics are a set of social, cultural, and political mores that construct and demonstrate the virtue of black womanhood through race work—the uplift of the black community toward a more equitable standing of blacks in America. Deborah Gray White argues that race work "became the means wherein black women could change their image, and from their point of view, the uplift of women was the means of uplifting the race."[12] Black clubwomen eagerly took on Mary Church Terrell's charge to "carry [their] burden in the heat of the day."[13] It was a burden steeped in Western constructions of femininity, for at its base was the insistence that the black woman's primary source of sociocultural strength was in the home. The leaders of the movement modeled classic ideals of feminine refinement for their followers. Terrell is described by one observer attending her speech on modern black womanhood as appointed in a "pink evening dress and long white gloves, with her hair beautifully done," and her bearing was deemed "regal."[14] Yet the women were always ready and willing to do the work necessitated by the demands of their community as more radical clubwomen successfully advocated for black women to move beyond the demands of the domestic sphere, insisting that "a woman's place is where she is needed and where she fit in."[15] I choose to connect the power of black women's respectability to the critical work of leading black feminist literary scholars of the late twentieth century.

At its most base level, black literary feminism grounds itself in (re)discovering and celebrating the rich histories black women of earlier generations.[16] The relationship between Alice Walker and Zora Neale Hurston, for example, demonstrates the crux of these ideas. In her essay collection *In Search of Our Mother's Daughters* (1983), Walker notes a particular kinship with Hurston and analyzes the looming influence of Hurston's life and literature in her own development as an artist. Walker's subsequent acts demanding Hurston's placement into the Literary Canon exemplify the actions of multiple black feminist writers and literary critics of the 1970s and 1980s.

The initial move in the grand project of bringing black women into the Canon was the establishment of a literary tradition of black women. The young critics who would lead the incorporation of this strategy became well versed in the literature, race work, and respectability politics of the black clubwomen from the late nineteenth and early twentieth centuries. Many early novels were written and published by the very same leaders and participants of the club movement. The authors of works examined by later black feminists read as a who's who of the club movement discussed in the previous section. *Invented Lives: Narratives of Black Women 1860–1960* (1987) by Mary Helen Washington features an entire section—Part Two—analyzing the fiction of prominent clubwomen Frances Ellen Watkins Harper, Pauline E. Hopkins, and Fannie Barrier Williams.[17] In Washington's critical introduction to Part Two, she exhibits confident knowledge of the shadow of the Cult of True Womanhood as the women "enlisted their fiction in the battle to counter the negative images of blacks and women."[18] Frances E. W. Harper's *Iola Leroy* (1892) is once again encountered in Barbara Christian's groundbreaking critical text *Black Women Novelists: The Development of a Tradition, 1892–1976* (1980). Christian contextualizes the importance of Harper's text by highlighting that it "so clearly delineates the relationship between the images of black women held at large in society and the novelist's struggle to refute these images."[19] Christian clearly recognizes the politic of black women's respectability embedded within the novel's social critiques. Similarly, the names of prominent advocates of respectability populate multiple chapters of the foundational text of black feminism, *All the Women Are White, All the Blacks Are Men, But Some of Us Are Brave: Black Women's Studies* (1982). This text, edited by Gloria T. Hull, Patricia Bell Scott, and Barbara Smith, gathers the critiques, bibliographies, and suggested black feminist course curricula by highly influential scholars theorizing and practicing black feminist theory across disciplines. Patricia Bell Scott's "Selected Bibliography on Black Feminism" suggests Anna Julia Cooper's *A Voice from the South: By a Black Woman of the South* (1892) as well as proto-feminist Maria W. Stewart's *Productions of Mrs. Maria W. Stewart* (1832) and prominent activist Mary Church Terrell's *A Colored Woman in a White World* (1940). Gloria T. Hull contributes a chapter that focuses on the life and works of Alice Dunbar-Nelson. The scholars discussed above—Barbara Smith, Mary Helen Washington, Barbara Christian, and Gloria T. Hull, as well as a few others—rose to prominence in part with their critical work on the clubwomen writers of the previous century.[20]

Respectability advocates vowed to revise the negative images of black womanhood as both writers and doers of the word in all aspects, writing fiction as well as fighting for suffrage. I suggest that the clubwomen's commitment to authorship, as well as their politics of respectability, impressed the black feminists researching their works almost a century later. I do not believe that the late twentieth-century scholars began living lives of utmost decorum with "not a hint of impropriety."[21] But I do insist that proto-black feminists' long-term strategies for the incorporation of black women into mainstream America constructed a blueprint for their descendants' approach for placing black women writers in the Canon by designing a new interpretation of respectability politics, inspiring a politics of literary respectability.

Literary respectability consists of a fluid set of practices— heavily influenced by the respectability politics of the club movement—incorporated by leading scholars of black feminist literature with the goal of collapsing the gendered racist and classist walls of the literary Canon. Literary respectability, derived from the respectability politics of their foremothers, was successfully integrated into contemporary academia by countering the negative images of black women in literature and presenting evidence of the historical invisibility of black women writers by proving their existence throughout American literary history.

The solution to the invisibility of black women's literature in university halls has been the development a cohesive black feminist literary theoretical framework as well as the procurement and development of black feminist scholars adept at reading, writing, and—most important—publishing their work on black women's fiction in scholarly journals and presses. Barbara Smith highlights "the necessity for nonhostile and perceptive analysis of works written by persons outside of the 'mainstream' of white/male cultural rule."[22] Smith demands the creation of a "space" for the "exploration of Black women's lives and the creation of consciously Black woman-identified art" while emphasizing the lack of political power that exists within the academy to make these spaces a scholarly reality.[23] In truth, *Toward a Black Feminist Criticism* is a call for the development and—most important—the organization of the political prowess to carve out as much space as necessary. In the end, the work is what matters, "for books to be real and remembered they have to be talked about. For books to be understood they must be examined in such a way that the basic intentions of the writers are at least considered."[24]

Barbara Christian chose to combat the lack of academic support and collegiality when scholars—particularly those on the tenure track—began to answer Smith's call to read, write, and publish criticism centering on black women's creative writing. Filled with a renewed commitment to the study of black women's creative fiction, Christian found a general sense of intransigence among her colleagues toward her research plan. Fellow scholars "warned me that I was going to ruin my academic career by studying an insignificant, some said nonexistent, body of literature."[25] Christian met true resistance in attempting to publish this work in scholarly journals and by university presses and found herself against the dangerously antiquated ideals of the academy: "Practically all academic presses as well as trade presses commented that my subject was not important—that people were not interested in black women writers."[26] The fight to establish black feminist literary criticism in academia was—and remains—a long, hard slog through academic detritus and pushback against the limited boxes white women, black men, and particularly black women's literature and criticism were allowed to occupy. Difficult decisions were made to ensure forward movement and protect what small area the scholars hewed for themselves, their subjects, and their work.

Black feminist literary scholars found themselves in the unenviable position of combating the troubling literary norms of the Canon even as they were committed to employing literary respectability to gain entry. Scholars began by questioning the very merits of being included, deliberating if "the thoroughly rationalist approach of European intellectual discourse might have seemed . . . to be too one-dimensional, too narrow."[27] The critics vowed to change the rules even as they evoked them, insisting that "black feminist criticism needed to break some of the restricted forms, personalize the staid language associated with the critic—forms that seemed opposed to the works of the writers as well as the culture they came from."[28] The scholars wanted to revolutionize the Canon from within, but the cost of entrance heavily mitigated the feasibility of true and substantial change. There existed a hyperawareness of the potential blowback of literary respectability as these authorities of black feminist thought were certainly aware of the pitfalls of compromise as they set guidelines to acknowledge the power of difference between the Western and the African as well as all the possibilities in-between: "All African-American texts are not the same. There are standards, not always the same as those upheld in the West, that African Americans hold to in determining what is the good and the beautiful."[29] Those standards, who would construct them and how they would be measured, created a space where the speculative could be dismissed and ignored by the literary theorists of that time.

Sycorax Haunts Black Feminist Literature and Theory

In this final section I begin to grapple with the legacy that black feminism leaves for future scholars of literature, particularly this project's focus upon horror in black women's creative works. The following chapters push past Christian's self-critiquing inquiry, "Can we think about how narrowly defined our own definition of scholarship might be?," to conduct a sustained scholarly pursuit of the dynamics of black woman–authored horror texts.[30] In the previous section, I articulated how a politics of literary respectability developed and defined itself within black feminist literary scholarship. I now want to center the specific implications the frameworks had upon the potentiality of horror scholarship in black feminist criticism.

I contend that the expectations set by the initial creators of black feminist criticism failed to consider the speculative fiction of black women writers as well as speculative analytical frameworks for those works they chose to privilege.[31] Speculative fiction simply did not fit with the critically thoughtful project of promoting the study of black women's fiction as valid academic research paths. Scholar Mae G. Henderson agrees, declaring: "There was certainly a privileging of certain writers among the 70s and 80s black literary feminists—after all, the project was then to establish a canon—or, at the very least, work to introduce black women's texts into an expanded canon."[32] The frameworks' leading scholars ignored the political potential of genre fiction—especially horror fiction and its themes—because of two interrelated reasons. First, they failed to recognize the intersectional potential of speculative fiction because of its assumed lack of gravitas. This action led to the dismissing of speculative and/or horror writers and theoretical frameworks active during the 1980s. Finally, horror literature lacked respectability— the scholars also did not want to be associated with the already ghettoized status horror possessed within Canon politics.

A narrow focus upon depicting the "lived realities" of black women by the early creators of black feminism left no room for the speculative, a genre of fiction rarely associated with either blackness or feminism. Horror author and critic Jewelle Gomez—a black lesbian feminist who sat on the editorial board of *CONDITIONS*, a lesbian literary journal—has always lamented this willful blindness: "It is the idea that speculative fiction is somehow an indulgence or that it is trivial that seems the most probable reason for its dismissal by literary critics as well as its lack of appeal to most Black readers or authors."[33] It is the incorrect assumption that speculative fiction could not forward the project of privileging black woman–centered literature that proved detrimental to the overall politics of literary respectability. It is not as if black women speculative writers did not exist within their contemporary community, for the speculative works by black women really began to make an impact in the 1980s, just as black feminist theory was being established in the academy. In her essay "Speculative Fiction and Black Lesbians" (1993), Gomez reads the writing of Cheryl Clarke—another politically active black feminist contemporary—and notes how her work incorporates themes of escape and slavery but also "insists on tying the past to the future."[34] Gomez expands her analysis to Michelle Parkerson and Barbara Buford. Gomez not only aided in privileging black women speculative writers, she was a poet and novelist in her own right, as seen in the publishing of her horror novel, *The Gilda Stories* (1990). The writing was nascent—just as the whole of black women's literature was at the time—but the knowledge and the works existed; they were either ignored or actively silenced. An interview with Jewelle Gomez reveals that Barbara Christian—Gomez's friend and colleague—initially discouraged Gomez's topical focus on a black woman who was also a vampire.[35]

The most egregious sin of black feminist literary scholars at the time remains their lack of engagement with the best-selling black woman writer of all time, Octavia Butler.[36] Walker, Christian, and other scholars decried the lack of published black women writers to study even as they failed to acknowledge a rising literary star who fit into their stated needs. In his essay "Why Blacks Should Read (and Write) Science Fiction" (2000), a direct reply to his earlier indictment of racism that populated science fiction in "Why Blacks Don't Read Science Fiction" (1978), black science fiction writer Charles Saunders notes Octavia Butler coming to the fore in 1978 and reaching the heights of popularity in the 1980s.[37] Saunders highlights her "readability" as he supposes she is "possibly attracting some of the same readers who enjoy Toni Morrison."[38] I further Saunders's supposition by questioning if Butler succeeded in attracting the readers of Toni Morrison, why was she then unable to attract black feminist scholars starved for black women's creative fiction? My question necessitates a return to Gomez's rebuke of black literary theory—and subsequently black feminist literary theory—to read speculative fiction as trivial. Gomez places the rejection of Butler and writers of her ilk squarely on the shoulders of literary critics, and "the need by some writers and readers for Black literature to serve a higher purpose—that is, to address racism directly—sometimes leads Black writers to ignore, to some extent, other issues."[39] The early scholars—misguided by literary respectability politics—missed fertile opportunities to engage with black woman–centered works authored by black women because of their inability to recognize the layers of nuanced identities permeating the works of Butler and her speculative sistren.

The prejudices against speculative fiction also account for the discounting of fertile research opportunities in the already privileged literary fiction of writers such as Toni Morrison and Gloria Naylor.[40] Earlier analyses of their texts focused on the lived realities of their central characters or were given the misnomer of magical realism. Magical realism is a theoretical framework gleaned from Latin American epistemes in which "we find the transformation of the common and the everyday into the awesome and the unreal. It is predominantly an art of surprises. Time exists in a kind of timeless fluidity and the unreal happens as part of reality."[41] I am certainly not declaring magical realism an inept theoretical concept—what I am stressing is that the framework does not fully address the racially gendered needs of black women's creative fiction. It is a theoretical hand-me-down that fits black women's literature, but not very well—it is in dire need of tailoring to its specific literary themes. I suggest that a racially gendered framework, grounded in horror theory, provides awesome research opportunities to contemporary black feminists.

I recognize that I am actively privileging horror theory over well-established and widely accepted analyses of magical realism as the cause of the inexplicable occurrences present in classic black feminist literature. I am not suggesting that horror replace all the other frameworks the following writers have been read through—I am simply arguing for the recognition and use of horror studies as a valuable framework in which to read these works. But black feminist theorists have consistently overlooked horror's almost commonsensical potential to explore the marvelous in our scholarly readings of black women's fiction. At its most base level, Toni Morrison's *Beloved* (1987) is a ghost story. True, themes of generational trauma, chattel slavery, and mother-daughter relationships are prevalent, but they all occur within the framework of a prototypical ghost story. Charles Saunders muses: "the strong supernatural element in *Beloved* could easily qualify it as fantasy, or, at the very least horror in the mode of Henry James' *The Turn of the Screw*."[42] The first eight to ten years of literary analysis of *Beloved* focused on ghosts and hauntings, but only spoke of these supernatural elements in terms of the "horrific" effects of slavery upon the psyche of the formerly enslaved. There were no readings of the ghosts and the possessed as traditional elements of horror and how Morrison employs them specifically within a black feminist dynamic—it remains incredible that so much genre potentiality was bypassed by the very creators of the discipline. Similarly, Gloria Naylor's *Mama Day* (1989) has yet to be fully analyzed within a horror framework. Often, black feminist studies of Naylor's work have focused on African American folklore, the power of Miranda Day as a conjure woman, and, lately, the presence of hoodoo spells and curses. There exists a lack of consideration of connecting the conjure woman to the Mambo in the sense of exploring the deep elements of horror that exist within Naylor's groundbreaking work.

Shakespearean themes suffuse Naylor's text—there is even the presence of the magical island of Willow Springs, not unlike the island ruled formerly ruled by Sycorax in *The Tempest* (1518). Once again, the absent presence of Sycorax and her potentiality as a black feminist figure of horror are ignored. Only this time women who reflect her own appearance disregard Shakespeare's black witch.

Horror was actively ignored as a research possibility because of the ghettoized status it held within the literary arts. Scholars were already wrestling with the vagaries of demanding that academic institutions include black woman–authored literature; they did not need the added taint of horror. Horror works—such as Mary Shelley's *Frankenstein* (1818) as well as Edgar Allen Poe's *The Raven* (1845)—are included in the literary Canon, but each has been ameliorated by the milder, more acceptable term as Gothic literature. Finally, the scholars at the time did not want to be associated with B-movie schlock. The struggle for academic acceptance took place in the waning years of Blaxploitation films centering on unreal characterizations of black women such as Tamara Dobson in *Cleopatra Jones* (1973) and Pam Grier in *Foxy Brown* (1974). Blackness and horror were still being heavily associated with superfluous and culturally problematic films such as *Blacula* (1972) and *Scream Blacula Scream* (1973).

In the end, Sycorax haunts black feminist theory just as forcefully as she haunts the mainstream horror explored in the first chapter of this work. Luckily, we can learn from the mistakes of early black feminist critics and use their guidance to fill the lacunae they left unexplored for their own political reasons. In the following chapters, I take note from the revisionary potential of black literary feminisms to place black women at the center of my inquiry into horror. This project builds upon Barbara Christian's acceptance that subsequent scholars would commit to projects that may prove "incomprehensible to our sense of what scholarly enterprises should be about."[43] In exposing such a lacuna in black feminist literature, the next two chapters are committed to articulating holistic theories of black woman–authored horror texts.

3

Black Women Writing Fluid Fiction

An Open Challenge to Genre Normativity

What we need to learn is what are useful and efficient
distinctions and what are inefficient and useless.
—Samuel Delaney, "The Second Law of Thermodynamics"

They take you and put you in one ghetto over another. You can
be a horror writer, you can be a fantasy writer, you can be a science
fiction writer—but you can't be them all. You have to choose one.
—Chesya Burke

This chapter discusses the fluid lines between horror, fantasy,
science fiction, and speculative fiction and how contemporary
black women genre writers exploit the obfuscation of these lines
to articulate the simultaneity of oppressions that uniquely affect
black women. Weakened distinctions between science fiction, fantasy, and horror create a genre confusion concerning black female
authors because few to none have taken the time to explore how
black women writers worry the lines between these genres to create a blend of horror/fantasy/science fiction that is specific to their
themes and analytical needs.[1] Confusion remains on this subject in
mainstream literature, and the complex identities of black women

often complicate an already labyrinthine genre discussion in writing what I term "fluid fiction."

I analyze black women writer's participation in genre literature throughout this chapter in three distinct parts. I begin by exploring the seeping lines in contemporary genre definitions of science fiction, fantasy, and horror and attempt to discern how black women writers refuse to squeeze themselves into these limited ideals. Next, I dispute the placement of these black women creators into the categories of speculative fiction and Afrofuturism while arguing for a subgenre that is explicitly black and female. I end this chapter with my contention that many contemporary black women genre writers exploit the clouded genre lines for their particular literary means by writing fluid fiction as elucidated in Nalo Hopkinson's *Sister Mine* (2013).

Genre Confusion

Confusion about genre definitions is not a new concept, and it certainly is not specific to black women who write genre fiction. The Library of Congress's Collections Policy on genre literature claims "the distinctions between science fiction and various other subgenres of fantasy [under which they include horror] are indeed blurred at times and usually artificial."[2] In fact, "many authors in the genre frequently cross these artificial barriers in mid-work."[3] I discussed the difficulties associated with defining the horror genre in the Introduction, and I choose to continue using the simplistic, yet nonspecific definition offered by horror studies pioneer Robin Wood, "When Normativity Is Threatened by a Monster (or the Other)."[4] Though problematic—as all genre definitions are—Wood's statement offers the flexibility needed to create a large-scale discussion of genre. Though the following discussion is, at times, frustratingly amorphous with increasing amounts of pliability between the definitions, it remains necessary in order to approach the pressing need for my fluid fiction framework presented later in this chapter—a theory that brings a crucial specificity applicable to the genre writings of contemporary black women.

The Library of Congress explicitly states that fantasy "usually requires a willing suspension of disbelief."[5] The document continues with a description of characteristics of subgenres of fantasy:

1. [They] adapt, rework, or provide an alternate telling of myth or folktale.
2. [They] involve an alternate reality or alternate universe.
3. [They] rely on a displacement of time or space.
4. [They] make use of elements of the horrific, supernatural, paranormal, or the occult.

It is clear that the Library of Congress has chosen to incorporate a popular critical organizing tactic of determining fantasy to be a metagenre under which includes both horror and science fiction. Though a sensible organization of these three genres, it remains problematic in its equivocal lack of clarity.

Such an imprecise definition of fantasy allows for the above criteria to also define the horror genre. Many horror texts—such as F. W. Murnau's *Nosferatu* (1922), John Landis's *An American Werewolf in London* (1981), and George Romero's *Night of the Living Dead* (1968)—adapt and revise myths and folktales of vampires, werewolves, and zombies. Authors such as Laurell K. Hamilton— the Anita Blake: Vampire Hunter series (1993–), Jonathan Mayberry—the Joe Ledger series (2009–), and Christopher Farnsworth—the Nathanial Cade series (2010–) create alternate realities in which demons, vampires, werewolves, fairies, and zombies exist and must be bargained with and/or destroyed. Stephen King's dome found in *Under the Dome: A Novel* (2009), the sewer system from *It* (1987), and the Overlook Hotel in *The Shining* (1977) are all physical structures that pause, disrupt, or conflate both time and space. Finally, elements of the supernatural, the paranormal, and the occult populate the horror genre—a splendid example is the trope of the haunted house. Stephen King's *Salem's Lot* (1975), Tananarive Due's *The Good House* (2003), and

Jay Anson's *The Amityville Horror* (1977) are all novels in which a house becomes the embodiment of evil.

The document continues on to define science fiction by building upon its already tenuous organization of the fantasy genre—here, nebulous lines become even hazier. The Library of Congress defines science fiction by stating that it contains all of the criteria listed above to define fantasy as well as the following:

1. It is speculative in nature.
2. It assumes change as a given.
3. It projects a story-line into the future or into an alternative reality or history.
4. It explores a problem in technology, culture, philosophy, etc. beyond its current state.
5. It presents an atmosphere of scientific credibility regardless of the reality.[6]

Next, the text initiates a short list of what science fiction is *not*—or at least some of it is not. The policy insists that not all science fiction:

1. Takes place in the future.
2. Involves space travel.
3. Describes technology beyond current reality.
4. Deals with alien cultures.[7]

The policy finally notes: "these elements are common in this subgenre [of science fiction] and uncommon outside of it,"[8] thereby undercutting whatever strengths of delineation attempted in the establishment of the above criteria. It is necessary to note that the definitions outlined by the Library of Congress are not incorrect; it is simply that the blended nature of these three genres—science fiction, fantasy, and horror—increases the difficulty in enunciating a consistent definition of one of the genres.[9]

These genre definitions are deeply entangled with many theorists, writers, and fans attempting to unpack these terms by constructing their discussions against each other to highlight what each subgenre is not. Creator, writer, and producer of *The Twilight Zone* (1959–1964) television series Rod Serling discloses: "fantasy is the impossible made probable [while] science fiction is the improbable made possible."[10] Multiple Hugo and Nebula award-winning author Arthur C. Clarke maintains: "science fiction is something that could happen—but you usually wouldn't want it to. Fantasy is something that couldn't happen—though you often only wish that it could."[11] Note that horror is emitted from these discussions, denoting its ghettoized status even among the literati of the somewhat marginalized genres of science fiction and fantasy. Each of these sincere attempts to allocate meaning to science fiction and fantasy reaches the broadly amorphous nature of Robin Woods's declaration of horror as "when normativity is threatened by a monster." Again, I insist that the explanations of Serling, Clarke, and Woods are not incorrect—but each leaves the inquirer wanting more. Whether it is more specificity, more clarity, or more examples is unclear—but as both a critic and a fan, I am left somewhat bereft.

Other critics ascribe delineations of the genres by going deeper into each genre and constituting explications that become increasingly more specific even as they multiply the obscurity that accompanies these terms. The division of science fiction into "hard science fiction" and "soft science fiction" appears deceptively useful, but it ignores the seeping lines of crossover that remain common within the genre itself. Hard science fiction encompasses the use of one or more of the natural or physical sciences such as physics, chemistry, biology, geology, and astronomy. Soft science fiction deals with the science of humans and their behavior such as psychology, sociology, anthropology, and political science. Nevertheless, most science fiction texts are a cogent blend of both the hard and the soft sciences.

Stanley Kubrick's iconic science fiction film *2001: A Space Odyssey* (1968) craftily begins with a focus on the hard sciences—as astronauts initiate travel to Jupiter amid the stark, white minimalism of hard surfaces and furniture created through man's scientific advancements. There is an emphasis on the artificial genius of the mission's spaceship, the life-saving protection provided by space suits as the astronauts complete scientific experiments and prepare for the initial visit to such a faraway planet. The camera captures a mise-en-scene that is an orgy of structures and products made through breakthroughs in chemistry and biology—even as the mission itself is made possible by man's advancements in physics and astronomy to map out the geology of an alien landscape. Perhaps the film's most auspicious exemplar of man's scientific genius is the creation and inclusion of HAL 9000—the artificial intelligence program tasked with "perhaps the greatest responsibility of any single mission element. You're the brain and central nervous system of the ship."[12] Yet it is the study of human behaviors—the softer sciences—that provides the plot catalyst for the exploration of the film's central themes.

HAL 9000 evolves from a clever artificial intelligence apparatus into what he refers to as a "conscious entity"—he becomes "human."[13] It is HAL's misreading of humanity—for he can only experience humans through the distorted lens of the hard sciences—that originates in his creators' inability to sufficiently elucidate the intricacies of humanness investigated in softer sciences such as psychology, sociology, and anthropology. HAL's imbalance elicits his problematic augmentation of humanity—leading HAL to murder all but one of the ship's crew members, all in his inscrutable allegiance to completing the mission. HAL's inability to place humanity within its proper perspective tenders his nonchalance in overruling human authority and devaluing human life. Thus, *2001: A Space Odyssey* acts as a meditation upon the need for both hard and soft sciences to actualize a great science fiction story.

Arthur C. Clarke, one of the founding fathers of contemporary science fiction, craftily expands its boundaries by revising the understanding of science. Clarke believes that "magic's just science that we don't understand yet" while insisting that "any sufficiently advanced technology is undistinguishable from magic."[14] Clarke's reading of science instigates my discussion of the permeability of the walls between science fiction and fantasy—for magic often substitutes science as the purveyor of knowledge and solution to plot predicaments. Still, even fantasy has been subject to multiple internal divisions and squabbles similar to those that plague science fiction.

Most critics attempt to define fantasy by separating it from science fiction and horror before articulating the genre on its own terms. The *Encyclopedia of Fantasy* declares that fantasy "continues to lack the specificity of science fiction"; rather, fantasy is more of a structure, a form that differs from horror, "which is named solely for the affect it is intended to produce."[15] In their introduction to *The Cambridge Companion to Fantasy Literature* (2012), editors Edward James and Farah Mendlesohn coalesce many differing ideas of fantasy to set the stage for their edited volume. Fantasy writer and critic Brian Attebery proposes that "we view fantasy as a group of texts that share, to a greater degree or other a cluster of common tropes which may be objects but which may also be narrative techniques."[16] James and Mendlesohn acquiesce that the particulars of those tropes add up to what they term "'a fuzzy set' of fantasy," acknowledging the continuously murky nature of defining fantasy in particular and genre fiction at large.[17] The introduction continues by conceding to the idea that all fantasy texts are in conversation with each other even though a consensus on its canon and even its components fails to exist. The following consideration reinforces Sylvia Kelso's assessment that "what can now, ironically, be called 'traditional modern fantasy'—the work of Tolkien, Eddings, and Jordan—is distinguished, in a 'shopping list,' by the scenario of a pre-industrial secondary world, with the central mythos of a Quest and/or bildungsroman, and the equally frequent pattern of 'There and Back Again.'"[18]

Yet the failure to form a consensus does not prevent noted scholars from valiant attempts to delineate their beloved genre. In *The Encyclopedia of Fantasy* (1997), coeditor John Clute defines the genre of "full fantasy" as "the story of an earned passage from BONDAGE—via a central RECOGNITION of what has been revealed and what is about to happen, and which may involve a profound METAMORPHOSIS of protagonist or world (or both)—into the EUCASTROPHE, where marriages may occur, just governance fertilize the barren LAND, and there is a HEALING."[19] I want to follow through Clute's thematic definition as I examine N. K. Jemisin's fantasy novel *The Hundred Thousand Kingdoms* (2010), the first entry of her Kingdom trilogy. Jemisin is particularly noteworthy because she seamlessly coalesces classic European fantasy tropes with specifically non-Western cosmologies even as she centers the journey of a young black woman in her novel. *Kingdoms* revolves around its protagonist, Yeine Darr, a tribal chieftain eventually thrust into the dangerous politics of castle intrigue as she is invited to live in the city of Sky ruled by her grandfather, the King. Yeine finds herself a pawn between the power struggles between her royal family members and the pertinacious gods they have enslaved. Yeine's journey begins in BONDAGE, for she is the chieftain of the Darre people, a physically, socially, and economically marginalized matriarchy excommunicated by the larger society because her brown father fell in love and married the princess of the most powerful tribe in the land, the Arameri, bringing her to willfully abdicate her throne. Clute emphasizes that the initial stage of BONDAGE "is normally signaled in fantasy by WRONGNESS, by a sense that the world as a whole has gone askew, that the story of things has been occluded."[20] In *Kingdom*, the WRONGNESS comes with the death of Yeine's mother, Kinneth, and her suspicion that her mother was murdered on the order of her spurned grandfather, Dekarta, head of the Arameri family and ruler of the Hundred Thousand Kingdoms. The journey from BONDAGE to RECOGNITION also hinges upon THINNING, a "dangerous and painful . . . fading away of beingness."[21] THINNING "may manifest itself through the loss of magic or the slow death of the gods . . . or an Amnesia (the protagonist's, or the world's) about the true nature of the self or history . . . or of any of the consequences of the rule of a Dark Lord, whose diktats almost inevitably represent an estranging parody of just governance."[22] Multiple aspects of THINNING occur once Yeine accepts Dekarta's invitation to the city of Sky in which he declares Yeine the heir to his kingdom.

Dekarta's decree places her in danger from her twin cousins and from the enslaved gods planning an insurrection to the rule of the Skyfather, the god of light, the victorious god who condemns his brother, Nahadoth, the embodiment of darkness, and his fellow gods to be the slaves of his beloved Arameri. Yeine loses a sure sense of self to the castle intrigue of so many interested parties out to ensure her demise. Yeine comes to realize that she is quickly being groomed as a sacrifice to the Skyfather by Dekarta to ensure his rule and as a sacrifice to reincarnate as the goddess Enefa—who rules over dawn and twilight—and the only hope to restore balance to the universe and remove the chains of bondage from the gods, ensuring the kingdom's survival. Yeine becomes a symbol, her individuality and her very agency as a human being wither as she realizes that she may only be a vessel for Enefa—her conscious was placed in an amnesic state within baby Yeine to ensure her survival beyond the Skyfather's grasp. The final aspect of THINNING occurs with the realization that the Skyfather, the god of light and clarity, truly embodies the Darkness of the world, not Nahodoth. The Skyfather has hidden the dark nature of his crimes within the brilliance of his light, blinding all—particularly the morally compromised Arameri—to his evil and parodic sense of justice. RECOGNITION describes the moment at which the protagonist gazes upon the thinned world and achieves clarity of her journey's true purpose. It is only after this moment of transformative RECOGNITION that HEALING can occur, a transition often accomplished through literal METAMORPHOSIS.[23] Yeine's RECOGNITION comes with the realization that she was never meant to be an heir, only a necessary sacrifice to the Skyfather that allows true succession to the throne to occur. The moment of HEALING reveals itself with Yeine's acceptance and self-sacrifice as she dies to become the goddess Enefa. Yeine's literal METAMORPHOSIS into Enefa restores the balance of power between the world's light and dark for she regains her place as transition itself, the dusk and the dawn. My reading of both *2001: A Space Odyssey* and *The Hundred Thousand Kingdoms* reveals both the intense structure of genres as well as their fecund flexibility that sustains their popular and scholarly success. I use the next section to trouble the potentialities of such flexibility.

The Lacks of Speculative Fiction

The inception of theories such as intersectionality, multiplicities, and hybridity in the latter part of the twentieth century has led to a general acceptance of the difficulties in delineating clear definitions for the genres of science fiction, fantasy, and horror. These concessions generated a critical space that embraced the genres' incertitude, resulting in a new genre, speculative fiction. Speculative fiction has two working definitions in contemporary genre literature studies, with neither fully encapsulating its true intricacies. Speculative fiction began as a subgenre under science fiction literature and film that concentrates on "what if, if only, and if this goes on"—that is, to speculate.[24] In its contemporary iteration, speculative fiction has developed into a lackadaisical umbrella term for any fiction remotely related to genre literature. Another early scholar of contemporary science fiction, Robert Heinlein, views speculative fiction as including "all forms of fantastic fiction . . . science fiction, fantasy, and horror, supernatural fiction, apocalyptic and postapocalyptic fiction, utopian and dystopian, alternative history, and magic realism."[25] Speculative fiction's development into a catchall term for any work that mixes the genres of science fiction, fantasy, and/or horror proves its lack of usefulness for examining black women's genre fiction. Speculative fiction's unhindered growth and development power this chapter's urgent need to create and highlight a more distinct framework for reading black women's genre fiction.

The attempt to define speculative literature eventually becomes a question of what is *not* speculative fiction.[26] N. E. Lilly, from the speculative e-zine *Green Tentacles*, pushes the boundaries of speculative fiction even further by stating: "Speculative Fiction . . . also addresses works that are not science fiction, fantasy, or horror, yet don't rightly belong in other genres . . . [such as] fiction that includes Weird Tales, Amazing Stories, and Fantastic fiction.

It also may include other genres such as mysteries, Alternate Histories [such as Steampunk] and Historical Fiction."[27] Scholar Susanna Morris laments that speculative fiction "has largely been (mis)understood as a genre written only by whites (mostly men) about whites (again, mostly men)."[28] Poststructuralism shattered many misunderstandings about speculative fiction as non-white, non-male, non-heterosexual, and non-middle-class authors were reminded that the authors of science fiction/fantasy/horror consistently failed to make a space for Others in the literary ghetto in which their own work had been marginalized. It is within such a harsh reality that speculative fiction developed its allure, for it "is a term which includes all literature that takes place in a universe slightly different from our own. In all its forms it gives authors the ability to ask relevant questions about our society in a way that would prove provocative in more mainstream forms."[29] The inclusive nature of speculative fiction—particularly its ability to highlight the difficult social issues in a seemingly nonthreatening way—appeals to those who have been rendered outsiders in a literary framework constructed by those already excluded from the realm of literature. The umbrella of speculative fiction discounts no one; it accepts the gendered, the queered, the poor, and the weirdest of the weirdos. Yet I insist that in speculative fiction's sweeping inclusivity, the literary projects of black women become lost.

Black women authors do not currently eschew the label of speculative fiction even as I present its growing inadequacy as an efficacious descriptor of their work. Many of the black women discussed in this work have proudly published under its banner—Nalo Hopkinson, Tananarive Due, Nnedi Okorafor, N. K. Jemisin, Chesya Burke, and Kiini Ibura Salaam, to name a few. In a 1998 interview, Hopkinson declares: "I write fantasy (actually, I say 'speculative fiction,' because my work includes elements of science fiction, fantasy, dark fantasy, horror and magic realism)."[30] Prominent black feminist critics such as Gwendolyn Pough and Yolanda Hood devoted an entire issue of the *Femspec* journal to speculative black women in June 2005.[31] In their introduction, Pough and Hood focused on the need for black women to "create speculative visions of the world . . . [particularly given] black women's actual positions in the 'real' world as women who experience varying degrees of sexism, racism, and classism, and homophobia."[32] Most especially, the scholars propose the question, "How do current Black women speculate, rewrite, re-visit, and re-envision history in ways that connect them to Black women's legacies of struggle?," as the most important theme explored in the issue.[33] Pough and Hood's privileging of how black women "rewrite, re-visit, and re-envision" speculative fiction in their works elucidates exactly why speculative fiction proves inadequate. The very term "speculative" leaves the peculiar particularities of black women genre writers wanting, for it fails to explicitly acknowledge the deliberate nature of black women writers in blurring genre lines to articulate their "legacies of struggle" as dreams of the past/present/future.[34] Speculative fiction too readily glosses over author Nnedi Okorafor's insistence that "there is a method, purpose and realness to my madness. It is not fantasy for fantasy's sake."[35]

Sandra Jackson and Julie Moody-Freeman's editorial work in a May 2009 special issue of the journal *African Identities* parallels the ground-breaking work of Pough and Hood in *Femspec* by focusing on "The Black Imagination" and science fiction. Jackson and Moody-Freeman are perceptive in their recognition of the historical appeal of science fiction's, speculative fiction's, and fantasy's ability to act as social and political commentary on the Western world, particularly in their ability to highlight "geo-politics and conflict between nation-states as well as those between governments and their citizens, and responses to social, cultural, and technological changes."[36] The editors assert that black writers expand genre definitions by "appropriating" their "conventions" to "suit [their] own [authorial] needs, presenting new perspectives and posing questions not addressed in canonical works."[37] Yet I ponder, at what point does a specific faction of writers appropriate and adapt a genre so much so that it changes the very nature of a thing? Have black women creators breached the boundaries of speculative fiction so much that it has begun to collapse under the multiplicitous demands of black women genre writers? I certainly believe so. Within the dexterous machinations of black women creators, speculative fiction becomes more exclusive; it is raced, it is gendered, and it begins to steep itself in that which is labeled the African. Speculative fiction's flexibility becomes fluid, a fiction that roils and flows with purpose.

Race and Gender . . . and Genre

Many critics have proposed different frameworks and nomenclatures that recognize the racial and gendered gaps found in the oversimplifications of speculative fiction. Afrofuturism represents a successful articulation at recognizing the fluidity of science fiction and, to some extent, fantasy as viewed through the lens of race, for it is "speculative fiction that treats African-American themes and addresses African-American concerns in the context of twentieth century technoculture—and, more generally, African American signification that appropriates images of technology and a prosthetically enhanced future—might, for want of a better term, be called *Afrofuturism*."[38] Another critic, Mark Sinker, insists that the "central fact" of Afrofuturism "is an acknowledgement that [the] Apocalypse [has] already happened—Armageddon [has] been in effect."[39] The understanding of the contemporary postapocalyptic existence of Africa and its diaspora centers on colonialism and the transatlantic slave trade—that period of physical, cultural, and psychological loss was the Apocalypse. Afrofuturism has proven to be a shifting theory that centers itself on the relations between the African diaspora and science fiction/speculative fiction drawing from the most popular trope of the genre, exploring the very nature of being alien. Afrofuturism adopts this theme, which in its past has worked as a poorly disguised metaphor for discussing race—for example, James Cameron's *Avatar* (2009) in which the Na'vi, the race of blue aliens on the moon, Pandora, are a lazily problematic conflation of random indigenous cultures, and the actors voicing the Na'vi are all of African descent. Afrofuturism also acts as a reaction against the multicultural, "one-race" narrative of the future that actively erases blackness in a technological utopia.

"Afrofuturism" has become a term for all things black and genre-related (with the exception of horror). Many authors have been placed under its auspices, most especially Octavia Butler as well as Amiri Baraka, Nalo Hopkinson, Derrick Bell, and even Toni Morrison. The theory moves beyond the literary to encompass all manner of texts, from short stories such as Derrick Bell's "The Space Traders" (1992), Nisi Shawl's "At the Huts of Ajala" (2000), and W.E.B. Du Bois's "The Comet" (1920), to film, exemplified by Marcel Camus's *Black Orpheus* (1959), Ivan Dixon's *The Spook Who Sat By the Door* (1973), and even John Sayles's *The Brother from Another Planet* (1984). One of the most auspicious aspects of Afrofuturism remains its interaction with music texts; many of the diaspora's most interesting musical acts display fundamental elements of Afrofuturism, including but not limited to jazz composer Sun Ra, psychedelic funk originators George Clinton and the Parliament Funkadelic, as well as contemporary chanteuse Janelle Monae. These texts exemplify the range and multiplicities of Afrofuturism's existence as "a much more varied and complex set of relationships between domination and subordination, whiteness and color, ideology and reality, technology and race."[40] The question then arises, is the articulation of Afrofuturism applicable to the genre writings of the black women examined in this project? Where is the critical need for another term, another framework, and one more neologism? For all of its successes, the Afrofuturistic paradigm reveals two specific apertures: it possesses a myopic focus upon the future that fails to encompass a full engagement with its African past, and this myopia possesses an overpowering influence of science fiction.

My investigation of Afrofuturism begins by highlighting that the theory grounds itself in the notion that those of the African diaspora are a dispossessed community "whose past has been deliberately rubbed out, and whose energies have subsequently been consumed by the search for legible traces of its history."[41] For Afrofuturism, the African diaspora exists without a history significant enough for a deep engagement. Admittedly, the framework has displayed a certain affinity for Egyptian themes in many of its visual texts—but I read this engagement as perfunctory and at best performing the service of aligning blackness with an already established acceptance of the superior intelligence and futurist thinking of Ancient Egypt.[42] Afrofuturism's insistence upon a logic of ahistoricity is simply without merit. But a framework of blackness that cleaves from its past—occupying a postapocalyptic/postslavery dialectic—provides room to fixate upon the future.[43] Kodwo Eshun insists that Afrofuturism is "concerned with the possibilities for intervention within the dimension of the predictive, the projected, the proleptic, the envisioned, the virtual, the anticipatory and the future conditional." Eshun refers to this intervention as a chronopolitical act that allows "black artists, musicians, critics, and writers [who] have made . . . the future, in moments where any future was made difficult for them to imagine."[44] In truth, Afrofuturist frameworks center themselves on multiple disruptions to the fallacious linearity of time—but for my critical purposes, their specific point of intervention, transatlantic slavery, is already too far into the future. I insist that the authors studied in this text begin their intervention in precolonial Africa, thereby changing the implications and understanding of what is truly considered African.

Afrofuturism has consistently made an effort to be gender inclusive in expressions of its values. *Afro-Future Females: Black Writers Chart Science Fiction's Newest New-Wave Trajectory* (2008) exists as a successful attempt to examine the intersections of race and gender within the context of Afrofuturism even as it fails to fully account for the multiple ways in which specific black women authors are redenominating the genre. Scholar Marlene S. Barr begins by chiding Mark Dery and the framework's initial masculinist preponderance, but she also uses this weakness as an opportunity for her volume to explore the gendered renderings black women offer to the field. Barr's volume demonstrates a significant contribution to the growing field of black woman–authored genre content as she offers new original texts as well as innovative analyses of the most contemporary works by dominant critics in the field. I again find an inability of Afrofuturism—even in this iteration focusing on black woman–authored content and critique—to account for both the genre dexterity and the historical literary implications of authors such as Nalo Hopkinson, Gayl Jones, and Nnedi Okorafor. Barr's framework revision remains within the limits of science fiction, thereby failing to encompass the genre movements and conflations present in the authors' works. Though there are fleeting mentions of fantasy and, to a lesser extent, horror, Barr's primary concern is to expand science fiction. The volume's introduction reveals Barr's stated goal to "indicate the ways in which science fiction should be reconceptualized" through the study of Afrofuture females.[45] Unfortunately, Barr's myopic visions of revitalizing science fiction are incapable of encompassing and fully explicating the complicated nature of black women's genre fiction. My intent is to push Barr's initial ideas further, for it is my contention that these creators are simultaneously revising multiple aspects of genre fiction even as they reconceive notions of black feminist prose as a whole. Afrofuture females are consistently referred to as a new phenomenon, again revealing the framework's apertures concerning the past. The previous chapter of this text elucidated how genre-bending authors of this chapter are decidedly placed within the lineage of black feminist literary history. In the end, Afrofuturism's gender troubles, coupled with its lack of deep engagement with the past in which "it is easy to lose track of history," demonstrate its inability to account for the oscillating nature of black women writers' purposeful play with genre, blackness, and gender construction.[46]

Fluid Fiction

Fluid fiction is a racially gendered framework that revises genre fiction in that it purposefully obfuscates the boundaries of science fiction/fantasy/horror writing just as black women confound the boundaries of race, gender, and class. Fluid fiction develops from complex aesthetic traditions that derive from a literary homeplace constructed by black women genre writers. Homeplace, bell hooks articulates, is a place far away from the Western world's objectification of blackness and creates a safe space in which black men, women, and children become subjective beings of agency.[47] I extrapolate from hooks's theories of homeplace, radical black subjectivities, and black feminist aesthetic theory to argue for black women genre writers' determination in creating a literary homeplace from which fluid fiction flows. I assert that fluid fiction is the result of black women's fight for literary subjectivity within genre fiction and that black women writers act as a destabilizing force for problematic genre delineations that too often render them invisible and silent. I center my textual analysis of fluid fiction on the genre-thwarting oeuvre of Nalo Hopkinson, whose work stands as an exemplar of the tenets of fluid fiction. As the result of the politically liberatory act of hewing space for gendered black genre literature, fluid fiction becomes what writer Samuel R. Delaney terms "a useful and efficient distinction" in which black women articulate themselves under their own terms.[48]

Literary homeplace describes a constructed intellectual space of subjective freedom and resistance created and maintained by black women genre writers. In this space of self-revelation, black women creators are freed from the constraints of literary respectability politics in which they must always be concerned with larger black feminist goals of being deemed writers of literature.[49] Here, authors are encouraged and given the agency to be different, to play with genre as they incorporate expressions of their raced, gendered, classed, and sexual identities. bell hooks suggests that participants in homeplace "are working to make spaces where black women can dialogue about everything, spaces where we can engage in critical dissent without violating one another."[50] It is in such a space that an author such as Nalo Hopkinson can produce a story in which a heterosexual couple uses the technological wonders of a body suit that acts as a pleasure aid that allows them to switch sexual organs. The pleasure found in exchanging nooks and crannies and Cleve finding "out what it feels like to have a poonani" is celebrated as a sexy voyeuristic fantasy of the reader to discover the intimate pleasures found in long-term monogamous relationships.[51] Within this homeplace, Hopkinson grabs the opportunity to do the unexpected, to develop Cleve and Issy's cries of pleasure into pain as the story detours into science fiction horror—the Senstim Co-operation's wetsuits take on a life of their own to become dangerous ganger balls of electricity once carelessly discarded by the couple after coitus. In the midst of the dangerous doppelgänger of sexual lightning threatening both characters, Hopkinson brings the reader back to the essence of love as the danger is destroyed through a combination of improved communication between the lovers and the strength of touching each other, skin to skin. I again stress that only within a racially gendered community of safety and psychosocial inner peace can Hopkinson feel so open to express her black woman weird—because ultimately the construction of literary homeplace is about self-recovery and developing the strength to push back against the static notions that bind black women's creative genre fiction. A literary homeplace goes beyond the figuration of peace, for its most powerful element remains its existence as a "site of resistance" against multiple hegemonies. Literary homeplace sustains an antagonistic relationship toward the hegemonies of the white patriarchal constructions of literature that mark Canon formation, the white patriarchal constructions of genre literature that is marginalized by the Canon, as well as the black feminist literary hegemony that forced its way into the Canon and perpetuates misguided ideas of what constitutes black women's literary expression.

The fluid fiction produced in this homeplace offers black women creatives the freedom to explore multiples aspects of black feminist theories within a literary context without being bound by privileging of the lived realities of black women and literary respectability politics, early concerns of black feminist literary theory. In "Ganger Ball Lightning," Hopkinson demonstrates common issues located within black sexual politics between heterosexual couples, including emotional mistrust, perpetuating damning sexual stereotypes of each other, and the need to reach a healthy place of maturity, healing, and support for success.[52] For in order to truly reach out and touch each other's skin—therefore banishing the electronic ganger endangering both of their lives—Cleve and Issy must admit to their emotional insecurities with the same vigor in which they revealed their deepest desires as they wore the pleasure suits. Cleve and Issy's love finds root as Cleve sacrifices himself to the ganger and discloses that he does not believe himself to be special to Issy: "If I'm not there, there's always sugar, or food, or booze. I'm just one of her chosen stimulants."[53] Issy's surprise at Cleve's openness spurs her to call the ganger to pay attention to her as she confesses her dislike for the suits because all she ever wants is to feel him, "Some heat. Some feeling. Like I show you. Like I feel. Like I feel for you."[54] Hopkinson's writing reflects Collins's sociological concerns in a fascinating way that encompasses the complications and multiplicities of black womanhood, particularly here within a couple's emotional catharsis when Cleve quietly concedes the real reason he purchased the technological wonders of the pleasure skins: "The only time we seem to reach each other now is through our skins. So I bought something to make our skins feel more, and it's still not enough."[55] As Issy finally understands why he had "started looking so sad all the time," she ignores the danger of the ganger and reaches out to touch Cleve, her love. It is only then that the ganger overloads and disappears with a popping sound. As the couple lay exhausted on the floor in each other's arms, Cleve deduces that they canceled the ganger out by touching each other and touching it, "we neutralized it."[56] Hopkinson demonstrates that black women's truths can be explored outside the harsh nature of reality, that indeed the fluidity of genre proves to reflect black women's reality just as effectively. It is necessary to note that even as Hopkinson subverts some of the more constricting black feminist literary ideals, she is still in conversation with the tradition by centering black womanhood and their unique experiences. Fluid fiction demands that black feminist literary theory expand to meet it on its own terms or leave a growing coterie of black women authors behind.

Fluid fiction writers are also a destabilizing force to mainstream genre fiction, for the authors' insistence on suffusing their work with a radical black feminist subjectivity openly challenges the limitations genre has historically placed on racially gendered inquiries. hooks insists that "assimilation, imitation, or assuming the role of rebellious exotic other are not the only available options and never have been."[57] Black women genre writers refuse to be what genre fiction expects of them as they consistently fight invisibility and are becoming a notable presence only under their own terms. It must be noted that their refusal is not simply an oppositional stance; hooks refers to opposition as "low-hanging fruit" and far too simplistic a notion to comprehend all that is black women's genre fiction. Literary homeplace and its resulting product are never still, for destabilization never finds roots, the resistance of fluid fiction is constantly engaging, revising, erasing essentialism even as it incorporates alternative cosmologies, epistemologies, and ontologies. For hooks reiterates that "we must employ fluidity to speak for ourselves."[58] The gall to speak for themselves, to demand subjectivity in a genre fiction that refuses to adequately see them, must be understood as a radically political and liberatory act.

Fluid fiction allows black women creatives to seize subjectivity by consistently shifting the aesthetic framework of genre fiction as a whole. hooks proposes aesthetic theory as "a way of inhabiting space, a particular location, a way of looking and becoming," and it must be understood that the continuous changing nature of fluid fiction gives black women's literary subjectivity its power within genre.[59] These black women have worried the lines of genre to a point of almost infinite possibility as they incorporate their ontological space as shifting signifiers of identity. The subjectivity gained within fluid fiction actively subverts static notions of black, gendered, sexualized, classed, *and* genre identity, bringing forth previously inconceivable notions of self-actualization.[60] Fluid fiction becomes a necessary tool for confounding dominant hegemonic structures, for its fluidity removes opportunities of containment; its flexible shape always provides the opportunity to go under, around, and even over impediments to its movement. Referencing Audre Lorde in the introduction to her edited volume *So Long Been Dreaming:Postcolonial Science Fiction and Fantasy* (2004), "In my hands, massa's tools don't dismantle massa's house—and in fact, I don't want to destroy it so much as I want to undertake massive renovations—then build me a house of my own."[61] The subjective nature of fluid fiction offers a new "alternative habit of being and resistance" by heavily borrowing from non-Western, specifically African diasporic traditions.[62] For in order to properly read these authors' works, we must profoundly alter previous critical literary paradigms.

The powerful nature of the fluid model develops within the disjunctures of the already marginalized nature of genre literature. In her discussions on black mothering, Patricia Hills Collins describes disjunctures as those times and spaces in-between in which motherwork gets done. I move the term from the language of mothering to see disjunctures within a fictive context. Disjunctures, similar to lacunae, gaps, and interstices, have long been associated as places of power for black women and reveal the authority black women possess to "move out of their place."[63] It is in the interstices in which black women undertake the most dynamic work that best addresses the potent variations of their subjectivity. It is betwixt and between the interlocking hegemonical structures determined to dominate their concerns that the black woman genre author finds a respite to simply be and create within the literary homeplace. It is necessary to highlight that the concept of homeplace itself displays remarkable changeability. It is not simply one location but many that "accept[] dispersal and fragmentation as part of" their construction as a paradigmatic alternative to hegemonic forces.[64] Disjunctures are not only powerful places to build and maintain subjectivity, they possess effective political and cultural reverberations. It is the agency displayed in the authors' decision to choose the location of cultural production that is so incredibly subversive and empowering. The interstitial nature of being "part of the whole but outside the main body" provides black women genre authors a peculiar position with which to view the scaffolding that contributes to the false and vulnerable constructivity of hegemonic forces of cultural production. Disjunctures are places of powerful transformation. Fluid fiction presents a counterparadigm that encompasses the structural and immovable nature of staid binaries, flowing within and seeping into the exposed weak points of institutional structures. Nalo Hopkinson proves the radical possibilities found within fluid fiction.

The Fluid Fiction of Nalo Hopkinson

The literature of Nalo Hopkinson expresses the three significant features of fluid fiction by intentionally slipping between and conflating the genre boundaries of science fiction, fantasy, and horror, as well as centering the narrative on the women and cultures of the African diaspora; even the authors maintain a conversation with other fluid fiction writers as well as classic black feminist literature. Nalo Hopkinson has published across the textual spectrum, and I focus my analysis on two short stories, "Greedy Choke Puppy" and "A Habit of Waste" from her collection *Skin Folk* (2001) and her novel *Sister Mine* (2013).

Nalo Hopkinson has long been characterized as the leading voice in black women's speculative fiction and has rarely, if ever, spoken against this labeling of her work. Therefore, I am mindful of placing her work within an alternative paradigm, but I hope to evidence how fluid fiction is more appropriate as it provides a racially gendered theoretical foundation in which her works operate. Hopkinson is a child of the Caribbean; she was born in Jamaica, raised in Trinidad and Guyana, before spending a few decades in Toronto—home to the largest expatriate Caribbean communities in the world. All of her works worry the boundaries of genre fiction as they delineate and conflate different aspects of science fiction, fantasy, and horror, usually by troubling Western cultural mores with the interstitiality of Caribbean society. The stories and values of the Caribbean—a mixture of British, French, Spanish, and/or Dutch cultural structures heavily blurred through the morays of Indigenous and African diasporic identities—provide the lubrication that allows Hopkinson to flow through the categories of genre fiction. Previous critics have termed Hopkinson's literature as displaying characteristics of hybridity and/or transgressive in nature, but both terms fail to account for the oscillatingly forward motion of fluidity.[65] Hybridity is a complex mixture without motion while transgression stymies that motion, locking it into a crab-like movement across boundaries. It is only the concept of fluidity that encompasses the total possibilities of movement available to black women creators such as Hopkinson—back and forth, to and fro, side to side, up and down, diagonals and spirals—movement always within a continuous forward progression.

Her short story "Greedy Choke Puppy" blends elements of fantasy and horror as it revises the European horror fable of the witch—an old woman who feeds off of the young to remain youthful in appearance—and intertwines it with the French legend of the vampire into a retelling of the Caribbean folk tale of the soucoyant. The soucouyant, or ol' higue, is the "Caribbean equivalent of the vampire myth . . . [and] derives from the French verb 'sucer,' to suck. "Ol' Hige' is the Guyanese creole expression for an old hag, or witch woman."[66] The plot centers on a daughter of the African diaspora, Jacky, a humanities Ph.D. student increasingly anxious about her place on the other side of thirty without a steady partner and/or nuclear family. Her supposedly waning appeal to men haunts her deeply: "I get to find out that when you pass you prime, and you ain't catch no man eye, nothing ain't left for you but to get old and dry-up like cane leaf in the fire."[67] Jacky obsesses even as she genuinely attracts a smart, handsome, and affable Terry—whom she subsequently scares off by bringing up marriage barely two weeks into dating. Her grandmother's attempts to comfort Jacky's angst increasingly lack the power to soothe, as she advises "love will come. But take time."[68] Granny also endeavors to quell the heat of Jacky's growing jealousy of her pregnant and partnered friend, Carmen. Granny warns her that the women of their family tend to run hot—"hot for life, hot for youth"—and advises her to seek healing and patience through other ways of loving: "Love your studies, look out for your friends-them. Love your old Granny."[69] Yet hot tears slide down Jacky's face as she ponders the announcement of the birth of Carmen's son. Hopkinson steadily escalates the metaphoric association of fire and heat to Jacky's growing panic—that she will fail in fulfilling the sociocultural roles the hegemony demands of women she has dangerously internalized. Jacky's rising temperature parallels that of the soucouyant, whose psyche we experience in italicized first-person narration because it is literally a ball of fire:

"The soucouyant is usually an old, evil-tempered woman who removes her skin at night, hides it, and then changes into a ball of fire. She flies through the air, searching for homes in which there are babies. She then enters the house . . . and sucks the life from its [the child's] body."[70] Clearly, Hopkinson is shrewdly weaving African and European cosmologies both new and old to contribute to the fluid nature of her writing. Hopkinson brings to the fore her radical subjectivity by infusing fantasy's ability to revise and perpetuate old myths with horror's fascination with blurring the lines of death and life through the legend of the vampire and the fear of one's life essence being stolen to sustain that of another, supernatural being. I would go even further to suggest that "Greedy Choke Puppy" also functions as a work of soft science fiction hearkening back to Arthur Clarke's insistence that "magic's just science that we don't understand yet."[71] The science in this story is thinly veiled by folklore. There is a science to the magic that imbues this particular story, from the method of how the soucouyant enters the home—through bedroom windows and keyholes—to the strict guidelines of how to destroy the being—rubbing the inside of her discarded skin with hot pepper so that she is finally destroyed by the dawn's early light.

"Greedy Choke Puppy" continues to define fluid fiction as it centers its narrative on the epistemologies and ontologies of African diasporic women, placing it in conversation with established, canonical black women's literature. I suggest that "Greedy Choke Puppy" is in direct conversation with both Octavia Butler's "The Evening and the Morning and the Night" as well as Toni Morrison's *Sula* (1973) particularly in regards to the burdens and potential of maternal inheritance—those nonmaterial values, mores, and ways of being black women inherit from their mothers.[72] Butler's story focuses on a female protagonist, Lynn, living with Duryea-Gode Disease (DGD), a genetic ailment that causes its carriers to self-destruct by the age of forty.[73] The destruction begins slowly as sufferers begin to drift off into an emotional and psychological world of their own, eschewing interaction with other people. Ultimately the disease ends in a sudden infliction of violence upon themselves, and sometimes others, as the afflicted person begins to dig: "He began tearing at himself, through skin and bone, digging. He had managed to reach his own heart before he died."[74] Survivors are usually hideously scarred, "Her face was a ruin. Not only her eyes but most of her nose and one ear were gone. What was left was badly scarred."[75] The plot turns on the protagonist and her fiancé's discovery of his mother at the Dilg estate for those living survivors of DGD. Dilg is a property run by and for those with DGD, and the protagonist discovers her destiny to aid her people as she has inherited a specific phero-mone that enables her to control DGD's destructive tendencies through voice guidance and heavy suggestion. "It's a pheromone. A scent. And it's sex-linked."[76] What is most interesting about the protagonist's inheritance of both genetic disease and powerful hormone is that both are given power by her mother. The protag-onist is a double DGD, as both parents possessed DGD, but the power of the hormone she emits comes from her mother's genes: "women . . . inherit from their mothers but not their fathers. . . . When two irresponsible DGDs get together and produce girl children . . . you get someone who can really do some good in a place like this."[77] That, coupled with the fact that she is a female, gives her the opportunity to open her own Dilg estate in another area of the country, furthering the mission of DGD carriers to help themselves develop healthier coping mechanisms for living with the disease.

I contend that Hopkinson incorporates the maternal inheri-tance of heat and the dangerous possibility of becoming a sou-couyant in "Greedy Choke Puppy" as a moment of engagement for a literary conversation with DGD found in Butler's "The Evening and the Morning and the Night."[78] As a carrier of the hot blood that runs through the women of her family, Jacky has the potential to love fiercely and be a powerful force within the lives of those who currently love her as well as her potential husband. Likewise, experiencing the genetic malady of DGD offers Lynn great pos-sibility as a force of social and intellectual change. Lynn studies biology, as there is "something about our disease [that] makes us good at sciences," and later, Beatrice distinctly recommends that she study medicine: "You may be able to do a great deal of good."[79] Whereas Lynn is successfully able to develop her malady—particularly the fact that she is considered a double DGD—into a useful tool to sooth and lead those with DGD around her, as Beatrice notes: "You put them at ease. You're there. You . . . well, you leave your scent around the house. You speak to them individually. Without knowing why, they no doubt find that very comforting."[80] Still, Jacky is unable to come to such a peace, perhaps because she is able to fully accept the loving embrace of her community or even perhaps because she is partnered with Alan, who offers her a steady presence on which to lean.

I further suggest that Jacky's lack of partner and her subsequent emotional and physical destruction parallel that of the titular character, Sula, of Morrison's 1973 novel. Both Sula and Jacky are iconoclasts, struggling with the black community's sociosexual expectations of respectable black womanhood. Sula's story is well known; she is "an artist without form," a woman who enjoys sleeping with men—even white men—on her own terms and relishes her status as a single woman who belongs only to herself. Yet she is outcast because her singularity is read as dangerous by the black community because of her refusal to live within their strictures of decorum. The Bottom attempts to punish Sula through social and physical excommunication for her disregard of community mores. It is only the critical loss of her best friend and confidante, Nell, that leaves Sula truly bereft—to die alone and apart from the one person she deeply loves and understands. It is necessary to note that, for Sula, death itself is not a punishment—only a transition. And on the final page of the novel, Nell recognizes that she has been punishing herself by excluding Sula from her life in her final exclamation of "Oh Lord, Sula, . . . girlgirlgirl."[81] Hopkinson juxtaposes Jacky's destruction as punishment against Sula to continue the story's overall parable that black women must find a way to operate outside of limited social strictures for their happiness and prosperity.

Jacky's downfall comes specifically because of the actions surrounding a deeply held belief that her worthiness remains based upon her abilities to become a wife and mother. Even as a contemporary woman of education and some means—she is a graduate student focusing her research on Caribbean myths—Jacky is unable to fully distinguish herself from the problematic nature of community expectations for women. Jacky maintains a vested interest in defining herself by her lack of success at domesticity. Further, she buys into the notion that she must remain youthful in order to hold any viable appeal to men—a societal lie uncovered in her ability to attract and hold Terry's romantic interest. Hopkinson is careful in her construction of Jacky—we view her situation sympathetically because of her Granny's consistent love and attempts to help her talk through her fixation on what she lacks. Hopkinson wants the reader to see this as not a question of Jacky and her lack of willpower, but as a testament to the power of narrow societal roles to engross even the most intelligent and modern of women.

Death is Jacky's punishment as she chooses an amoral method of maintaining her youthful appearance and attractiveness—stealing the life essence from babies as a soucouyant. Hopkinson highlights that Jacky is not punished for her inability to let go of wayward notions of womanhood, for in giving her an everywoman appeal it is clear that any one of us can be Jacky and probably are struggling with redefining successful womanhood.[82] The reader commiserates with Granny as she laments the need to destroy her granddaughter for killing Carmen's newborn. For even as she awaits the destruction the morning sun will visit upon Jacky, Granny continuously articulates her love for her granddaughter—referring to her as "doux-doux" and declaring that "you is my life."[83] Jacky's life acts as payment for the life she took in her attempt to sustain a way of life she believed would never come to be.

Hopkinson's newest novel, *Sister Mine*, continues her talent for articulating the tenants of fluid fiction as it contains a narrative that oscillates between the genres of science fiction, fantasy, and horror even as it is centered on a daughter of the African diaspora. *Sister Mine* also manifests the final attribute of fluid fiction as its plot development consistently references classic black feminist texts such as Alice Walker's *The Color Purple* (1982) and Toni Morrison's

Beloved (1987). Protagonist Makeda and her formerly conjoined twin, Abby, are not only women of the African diaspora—they are direct descendants of the pantheon of West African gods/orishas as the daughters of the orisha of agriculture. The narrative is a bildungsroman that centers on Makeda's journey to truth and maturity as she seeks and solidifies her place within the complicated mysteries of her mystical family. Hopkinson's work incorporates science fiction through the rigid rules of magic that govern her family, and fantasy through Hopkinson's Africanist re-reading of the great journey, even as she incorporates horror by reimagining the African American folklore legend of the haint.

Earlier, I suggested that Hopkinson's short story "Greedy Choke Puppy" functions as a work of soft science fiction that hearkens back to Clarke's earlier insistence about magic and science. If her short story was simply a rough formation of this idea, Hopkinson's novel *Sister Mine* solidifies her refining of fluidly redefining magic as science fiction. Hopkinson's redefinition is an outright act of defiance; eschewing the subversive, she directly strips science—and the fiction associated with it—of its Westernity, its association with white, male, and capitalist power. Hopkinson removes science from its questionable privilege and esteem in the hegemony. *Sister Mine* insists on flowing forward by hearkening back to the ancient ways of power manifestation denounced and derided by the modernity of science. The novel's most potent use of ancient magic is the reimagining of the West African pantheon of gods.[84] Through the characters that populate Makeda's family, Hopkinson demands that science fiction recognize and exalt its African and Indigenous dimensions. The world Hopkinson creates is segmented and organized in a way that still allows for oscillations of identity. There is the world of the gods and demigods that compose Makeda's family and operate on a different spiritual plane. Makeda and her twin sister, Abby, are the result of an affair between their demigod father, Daddy Wood, and a human woman. Daddy Wood's egregious sin is in the act of actually breeding with what was considered the help, and he is consequently punished by his mother, Grandma Ocean, to live a mortal life on the earthly plane. His godliness—or in Hopkinson's language, his godsoul—is removed and buried in the roots of a great silk-cotton tree guarded by human stewards of the family. There is the also the world of the claypickens or humans who live on the earthly plane and are oblivious to the magic that suffuses their world. Complicating this binary are those humans who know of the spiritual world and operate as intermediaries between the two worlds. Often they are servants of the Family for generations whether it be guardians of the silk-cotton tree that contains Makeda's father's godsoul or as permanently chosen mounts for the pantheon. The character Suzy, mother of two and descendent of a long line of celestial stewards, has been placed in charge of guarding and tending to the tree, Yggdrasil: "Centuries her family had been in charge of the hoodoo tree. It was their old guys' branch of the eternal tree, the spine of the world's soul."[85] The dutiful and dangerous duties of being stewards to the celestials is explored in the second chapter as Suzy's family is placed under siege by Daddy Wood's godsoul, which has escaped from the great tree and manifested as a powerfully parasitic kudzu plant aggressively attempting to enter her home. It is here that we see another aspect of the stewards' service to the Family, Suzy's six-year-old daughter, Naima, has been chosen as "Mister Cross's ridden in this generation of their family" and is referred to as a "living telephone" responsible for the direct communications from the Family.[86] Naima is characterized as the ridden because builds off of the Vodou concept of the horse, an acolyte who is often mounted and ridden, like a horse, by the loa/god and is seen as its temporary incarnation: "the 'horse' communicates with the congregation through words and stylized dances, offering advice, becoming a conduit for healing and relishing the opportunity to be among its devotees."[87] The false binary between humans and gods becomes more complex with the addition of Makeda and her no longer conjoined twin, Abby, who are deemed semicelestial as they are mortals but gifted with special powers because their of their father's god-status. Matters are further complicated by a short series of sentences Hopkinson places in the first chapter: "They're [the Family] not really venal, that lot, just too big for their britches. They've been emissaries of the Big Boss for so long that they forget that they aren't gods themselves, just glorified overseers. But overseers with serious power."[88] Though Hopkinson never returns to this idea again, she makes it clear that even the gods aren't truly gods—or more specifically, not THE God—and are simply another set of servants gifted with unimaginable powers and set with the task to shepherd the humans.

It is this information that arms me with the evidence to ground Hopkinson's pantheon in the New World manifestations of traditional African religions—most specifically, Santeria and Vodou. Both religious frameworks are based upon the idea that the orishas/loas are emissaries and servants of the greater power of God—referred to as Oludumare, "also named Olorun and Olofi in Cuba," in traditional Santeria is the "earth's creator and is a remote being [who] is considered an inaccessible and omnipotent god who abdicates his powers to divine intermediaries."[89]

In *Creole Religions of the Caribbean: An Introduction from Vodou and Santeria to Obeah and Espiritismo* (2003) authors Margarite Fernandez Olmos and Lizabeth Paravisini-Gebert insist that Vodou is, at its essence, a monotheistic religion: "practitioners recognize a single and supreme spiritual entity or God—*Mawu-Lisa* among the Fon, *Olorun* among the Yoruba, and *Bondié, Bondyé,* or *Gran Met* (the Good God) in Haiti."[90] The most popular and familiar aspect of Vodou is its believer's service to "a pantheon of powerful spirits called the lwa. The lwa, also know as mystères, anges, saints, or les invisibles, provide the link between humans and the divine."[91] Hence a direct link is established between the syncretic religions of Santeria and Vodou and the Family of demi-gods or gods (with a small "g") that comprise Makeda's magical relatives. It is necessary to note that though Hopkinson's gods are rooted in the African, they proudly exhibit Indigenous and European influences that heavily shaped identity in the Americas and the Caribbean. For example, the great tree, Yggdrasil, is of Norse origin. Yggdrasil is the great mythological ash tree of life that supports the nine worlds of Norse mythology and its heavens.[92] Hopkinson insists her worlds push beyond the simplicities of black and white, for "there are African, European, Asian, and South Asian people there [in the Caribbean world in which she came of age], all with centuries-long histories of being in the Caribbean—not to mention the aboriginal cultures. . . . And all of those races and cultures have undergone and are undergoing a certain amount of mixing."[93] Religious and cultural syncretism—or the successful weaving together of at least two opposing religions and/or philosophies—is an incredibly important theme in the work, for Hopkinson privileges acknowledging and reveling in the multiplicities of her characters and the worlds in which they operate.

The novel's privileging of traditional African religions weaves throughout the characterizations of Makeda's family. The matriarch, Grandma Ocean—described as the original deity that bore the subsequent gods and goddesses that compose Makeda's father, aunts, uncles, and cousins—rules the family. Grandma Ocean's characterization is directly linked to the orisha Yemayá: "Grandma's province is the waters of the world, salt and sweet both."[94] Yemayá is not only the orisha of the ocean, she is the goddess of all bodies of water, and blue is the color associated with her presence. Yemayá represents the multiplicities of motherhood as she is often described as life-giving, nurturing, and loving, but she also manifests as a "fierce warrior that kills anyone who threatens her children."[95] Still, Hopkinson again displays her enjoyment of flowing through boundaries by adding one, almost fleeting description of the actions of Grandma Ocean's horse—she "flip[s] open a fancy yellow lace fan to cool her face with."[96] This minor observation reflects Hopkinson's unwillingness to heed all boundaries, even those rooted in the African. The fancy yellow fan is a celebrated characteristic, not of Yemayá, but of her sister, Oshun, the orisha of romantic love, seduction, and fertility who occupies the rivers of the world and reigns over the colors yellow and gold. Oshun often manifests as a young coquette who uses a yellow fan to flirt with and dance for those blessed with her presence. Though *Sister Mine* contributes to Hopkinson's lifelong authorial project of revealing the large influence traditional African religions have on Caribbean culture, this small observation reveals that even then she revels in the fluidity of identity characteristic of fluid fiction.

Makeda's family members reflect multiple orishas present in the West African pantheon. Her father, Daddy Wood, is a god of agriculture: "His talents are growing, grafting, and pruning."[97] Beyond his mastery as a gardener, Daddy Wood also attracts woodland animals, as the family's home was always filled with creatures large and small: "Living organisms liked to be near Daddy. . . . [The nursing home was] experiencing . . . squirrels clambering down the chimney, alarmed deer in the foyer . . . an intrusion of cockroaches."[98] Daddy Wood draws some of his characterization from the Vodou lwa Azaka—usually referred to as Kouzin Zaka—who "walks the earth as a farmer, beggar, and vagabond . . . who works with his hands and loves a simply, happy life."[99] Hopkinson develops the majority of Daddy Wood's characterization from Orisha Oko—"the master of agriculture, farming, fertility, and the mysteries associated with the earth, life and death."[100] The influence of Oko is seen in the character's spiritual and ontological conflation of life and death—Daddy Wood spends the majority of the novel in a coma with his godsoul embodied and on the run in an ever-expanding kudzu vine threatening to infect the earth's biodiversity with the parasitic plant named Quashee. Daddy Wood's escaped godsoul disturbs the Earth's balance and initiates Hopkinson's complicated plot machinations. Similarly, Daddy Wood's brother, interchangeably referred to as Uncle Jack, Leggy John, and Mister Cross embodies the lwa Papa Legba, also known as the orisha Eleggua. Makeda explains that her uncle Jack "is a ferryman between the worlds"; it is his responsibility to bring the dead to the other world and new life—babies—to this one.[101] Eleggua is the most important orisha because of this crucial role he plays as the guide between the two worlds. He remains the first orisha created by Oludumare and is the key to any communication between this earthly plane and the celestial one where the orishas reside: "Eleggua is the owner of all roads, crossroads, and doors. . . . He facilitates divination by communicating to and for the other orishas, and to Oludumare herself."[102] Papa Legba occupies a nearly identical role within the Vodou pantheon and, similarly, often incarnates as an old man with a cane. Hopkinson also incorporates aspects of Baron Samedi, a leading ghede—or spirit—of the dead known for his sharp, funereal dress: "[Uncle John] swirled his cape out of the way, dropped his gold-topped cane, and opened the long reach to welcome us. In her haste, Abby knocked his top hat off."[103] Here in Uncle John's characterization Hopkinson skillfully blends aspects of the popularized Baron Samedi—his top hat and cape—with the cane associated with the lesser-known but more powerful orisha/lwa most associated with death and/or transition, Eleggua/Papa Legba.[104] Hopkinson continues to play with the fluctuating identities of orishas with her characterization of Makeda's other uncle, General Gun, and his other manifestation—or camino—Uncle Hunter. Caminos, or roads, are the different avatars of an orisha here on the earthly plane: "each road has a slightly different temperament and is found in a different place in nature."[105] General Gun literally transitions into different caminos as Makeda speaks to him—for his characterization is grounded in Orisha Ogún. Ogún is a warrior god who fights against injustice against his peoples: "Ogún has the intelligence and creativity to invent tools, weapons, and technology. He is the father of civilization in many ways. . . . It was his tools and labor that cleared away the wilderness to build cities, homes and roads." When Makeda first approaches her uncle, his eyes are likened to cold iron even as "the General was wearing fatigues, a helmet, heavy laced boots. He was carrying a Kalashnikov."[106] Here, General Gun manifests Ogún Shibirikí, an "assassin who . . . is driven by bloodlust," as he curtly dismisses their questions as he turns his back to his twin nieces.[107] While turning his back, General Gun becomes Ogún Alagbede, the "blacksmith who crafts tools and weapons tirelessly at his forge."[108] Makeda describes the shift as almost instantaneous: "he turned his back on us and returned to forging red-hot steel on an anvil . . . his chest had gone bare. The sweat beading his dark skin flickered red, reflecting the incandescent metal he was working. Each upper arm was thicker around than both my thighs together. He pounded his hammer on

FIG. 7. *Ogun Rising* by Black Kirby.

the anvil in time with the beating of the palais drums. . . . I was pretty sure he wasn't making a ploughshare."[109]

General Gun continues to shift, first into an army information officer and then into a businessman in a suit. Our protagonist is more than aware of the multitudes that construct her uncle because she begins to refers to him/them as "the lot."[110] Suddenly, General Gun becomes Uncle Hunter as Hopkinson brings in another manifestation of the orishas, Ogun's close compatriot Ochosi.[111] Ochosi "is a skilled, stealthy hunter . . . who always hit[s] the mark with his arrow. [He] knows the wilderness better than anyone else and has mastered the art of tracking his prey and killing it while being totally undetectable."[112] Yet even as Makeda describes the figure as Uncle Hunter, he manifests a camino of Ogun. Uncle Hunter wears a "snappy suit" and carries a briefcase and a cell phone "clipped to his waist in a tasteful leather hard-shell case."[113] Uncle Hunter is also *Ogún Onilé*, the manifestation that "establishes himself as the king of new lands and is a benevolent chief."[114] Clearly, Hopkinson plays upon the concept of benevolence, for it is evident that Uncle Hunter's concept of benevolence literally depends upon whether one is a hunter or the prey. Reveling in the fact that he is truly in charge and is no longer beholden to the limits placed upon his killing prowess by Daddy Wood, Uncle Hunter basks in his mother's approval: "I've been doing his job just fine, haven't I, Ma?"[115] General Gun/Uncle Hunter becomes a metonym for the undulating genre motions of Hopkinson's narratives—though a minor character, his continual metamorphoses embody the fluidity of Hopkinson's textual methodology that the text is in motion.[116] *Sister Mine* smoothly changes caminos—or ways—from one genre demonstration to the other, conflating, separating, and subverting science fiction, fantasy, and horror as it unveils the potentialities Hopkinson's writing offers both black feminist and genre fiction.

Hopkinson continues to display fluid fiction in her redefining of fantasy within a black feminist framework even as her writing in *Sister Mine* takes advantage of the nebulous boundaries the genre shares with science fiction and horror. Nnedi Okorafor, a literary inheritor of Hopkinson, is also known for her racialized theory of the fantasy genre organic fantasy. Though not specifically gendered, organic fantasy does offer insight into how Hopkinson begins to revise the fantasy genre in a way that benefits and feeds into the subversive nature of fluid fiction. Okorafor describes organic fantasy as similar to general fantasy, for "it has the power to make something familiar strange."[117] Okorafor then qualifies organic fantasy as a genre that "blooms directly from the soil of the real. . . . It is the most truthful way of telling the truth. For me, fantasy is the most accurate way of describing reality."[118] Organic fantasy, and its purposeful play between the real and the not real, articulates how Hopkinson redefines fantasy for her own use—ultimately revising genre fiction itself into a fluid fiction literary framework. Hopkinson states her love for the potential inherent in fantasy: "I like the way that fantastical fiction allows me to use myth, archetype, speculation and storytelling. I like the way that it allows me to imagine the impossible. . . . I don't see science fiction and fantasy as just wishful thinking. . . . If black people can imagine our futures, imagine—among other things—cultures in which we aren't alienated, then we can begin to see our way clear to creating them."[119] As discussed earlier, Hopkinson grounds her fantasy in the shape-shifting reality of the Caribbean. *Sister Mine* is suffused with the traditional African religions that manifest in the Caribbean. The language of the characters is infused with the patois of the Anglophone Caribbean—words such as "claypickens," "horse," "doux-doux," and "haint." Hopkinson moves organic fantasy from Okorafor's Nigeria to the New World, the Caribbean, and its diaspora in Toronto.

Hopkinson similarly revises the genre of horror as she conflates it with science fiction and fantasy into fluid fiction. *Sister Mine*'s revision of mainstream horror is most evident in its presentation and treatment of Makeda's haint. Haint is a popular aphorism for a ghost, particularly an evil spirit in African American—specifically southern—folklore and colloquialism. It is a linguistic revision of the word "haunt," or ghost. Hopkinson's use of the term "haint" is particularly noteworthy. In previous texts—such as *Brown Girl in the Ring* (1998), *Skin Folk* (2001), and *The Salt Roads* (2003)—Hopkinson refers to ghosts with the decidedly Caribbean term "duppy." I suggest that this development is purposeful as it demonstrates one more culture feeding into the shifting influences of this text's primary cosmologies. The use of the word "haint" acknowledges the significance of African American influence, just as Yggdrasil nods to her world's European influence.

Makeda's haint revises the horror trope of the ghost by making it a corporeal being that is able to attack her at almost anytime and anywhere. Hopkinson's choice is so pronounced because ghosts are usually tied to a particular area and often hindered in their purpose due to their lack of mobility. Makeda's haint is unhindered by such qualms; it attacks her any time she is vulnerable and alone, such as at the wooded lakefront where we are first introduced to the being that has the ability to cause physical harm: "I felt the scrape of claws slicing through the fabric of my jeans as I pulled away. My haint was upon me. Its small, heavy body scrambled, quarrelling, up my side. Hideously contorted baby face, brown as my own, its hair an angry, knotted snarl of black. No it had those large hands at my throat."[120] The baby monster Makeda describes is not a poltergeist, nor is it simply a psychological disturbance associated with the unease of a particular place; this haint is an imminent physical threat. Typical of ghostly horror, the haint is a fearsome thing—Makeda speaks of her terror, she screams at its appearance and bleeds with its vicious attacks—placing it squarely within the horror genre. Makeda's encounters with the haint become increasingly heinous battles for her very life: "I tore it off me and swung it around, full weight, to crack it with a dull thud against the bole of a tree."[121] Hopkinson allows the reader to be comfortable with reading the haint as a ghost on steroids, and then she upends her own dynamic. In actuality, Makeda's haint is her own mojo/godsoul that was removed from her body as a child by her uncle Leggy Jack on the order of Grandma Ocean. Her haint hasn't actually been haunting her to inspire terror, but to reincorporate itself into its rightful host—Makeda. In the end, Makeda's discovery of the true nature of her haint integrates this classic horror trope with the science fiction of the West African pantheon and the unreal realities of the organic fantasy, ultimately demonstrating a major tenet of fluid fiction—the conflation and oscillation between science fiction, fantasy, and horror.

I end my analysis of *Sister Mine* through the fluid fiction framework by demonstrating how the text is in dialogue with classic black feminist literature. *Sister Mine* possesses the intensely fraught and complicated relationship between sisters, leading me to conclude that Hopkinson is in direct conversation with the short essay "From the Poets in the Kitchen" (1983) by Paule Marshall.

I have discussed Hopkinson's unique talent for incorporating Caribbean language use and rhythms throughout this section's analysis of her selected works—how she incorporates Creole words such as "doux-doux" and "claypicken." Hopkinson's talent and interest as a wordsmith places *Sister Mine* in the midst of a linguistic conversation popularized by the kitchen table poets that dominate Marshall's short, critical essay. Both daughters of the Caribbean, Hopkinson and Marshall concern themselves with the power that creole languages imbue in women who have emigrated. Marshall describes her mother and her girlfriends as poets sitting at the family's kitchen table whose breadth of discussion and linguistic acrobatics "functioned as an outlet for the tremendous creative energy they possessed. . . . The[ir] need for self-expression was strong, and since language was the only vehicle readily available to them they made of it an art form—in keeping with the African tradition in which art and life are one—was an integral part of their lives."[122] Hopkinson takes the mimetic ideas explored in Marshall's essay and brings them to her fantastical worlds built around the lives and journeys of daughters of the diaspora—Makeda and Abby— whose characterization as artists, quilter and singer, respectively, reflect the Africanized language expression found in Marshall's piece. Hopkinson steadfastly believes in expressing the importance of the Caribbean identity of her characters and insists that "a lot of Caribbean identity is bound up in language. We have used it as a tool of resistance and politicization."[123] The women of Marshall's piece agree, proclaiming: "In this man world you got to take yuh mouth and make a gun!"[124] Marshall highlights the intricacy of the daily linguistic feats performed by her mother and friends—and it truly was a performance, for style was just as important as content: "They had take[n] the standard English taught to them in the primary schools of Barbados and transformed it into an idiom, an instrument . . . changing around the syntax and imposing their own rhythm and accent so that the sentences were more pleasing to their ears. They added the few African sounds and words that had survived, such as the derisive suck-teeth sound. . . . And to make it more vivid, more in keeping with their expressive quality, they brought to bear a raft of metaphors, parables, Biblical quotations, sayings and the like."[125] Hopkinson's respect for and use of Creoles allows her to fully represent the complexities of her characters and their Caribbean identity, for she states: "Creoles carry their own nuances and textures of meaning. . . . Every nook of every region of the English-speaking world tailors English to suit itself. That's one of the strengths of the language—its flexibility."[126] It is this flexibility that brings reality to the fluid fiction of Hopkinson's fantastical oeuvre. In the following chapter, I expand the flexibilities explored by Hopkinson's rendition of fluid fiction to provide a deeper understanding of black women horror writers. These women build upon the potentialities and liberatory actions of fluid fiction to redefine the very nature of horror, placing it in an Africanized folkloric context ripe with subversive abilities to challenge mainstream horror writing as well as black feminist literary theory.

4

Folkloric Horror

A New Way of Reading Black Women's Creative Horror

Critiques originating in black feminist thought, then, have had
a sure effect on the restructuring of traditional disciplines.
—Barbara Christian

A lot of my work begins in horror.
—Nnedi Okorafor

The dead are not dead.
—Dr. Bonnie Barthold

At the climax of Bree Newsome's short film *Wake* (2010), the black woman protagonist, Charmaine, rushes through the woods in her nightgown, hair unbound with harried, furtive glances behind her in the morning light. Charmaine's world has crumbled around her—her father is dead, and she suspects her recent husband to be a special kind of evil and possibly inhuman—so she runs to what she believes is the source of her problems, the death spirit in the woods. Charmaine's current temperament is markedly different from the cool confidence she possessed when she first met the otherworldly death dealer. Days earlier, Charmaine strolled determinedly single-minded in her purpose to conjure a man. Charmaine was calm, collected, and prepared. She carried a conjure box, filled with the likeness of the man of her dreams—deep mahogany skin, a handsome figure in a sharp white suit, and piercing green eyes—as well as trinkets of affection and a few bones signifying the sacrifice of small animals for the exchange of *ashe*, or life spirit, a necessary element to bring forth life in root work.[1] So far, the narrative had only hinted at the largest sacrifice Charmaine has given to become a wife and mother, "A man? Well, you gotta give one to get one!" the ghede embodied in a honey-colored woman dressed in a voluminous red and black dress from a previous century.[2] Charmaine eagerly proffers a handkerchief full of dirt from her father's fresh grave. "How'd your Daddy die?" the woman-spirit slyly inquires.

Wake demonstrates the rich potential for the horror genre to successfully examine the social anxieties that often plague contemporary middle-class black women. The twin forces of respectability politics and a supposed dearth of ideal black men have contributed to working single black professional women into a frenzy of spinsterhood or worse, single motherhood with little to no hope of love and wedlock—the only avenue to happiness if black middle-class values can be believed. Such fears occasionally

FIG. 8. Buena Batiste Webber as The Demon, *Wake* (2010).

spike into the cultural consciousness, with its last peak seen in the early 2010s characterized by such titles as Ralph Richard Banks's *Is Marriage for White People? How the African American Marriage Decline Affects Everyone* (2011). Charmaine has been pushed to act because she fears the social consequences of becoming an old maid as articulated by the trio of older women gossiping about her life at her father's burial: "Charmaine passed the old maid mark a while ago if you ask me. She's just lucky her Daddy died when he did . . . while there's still time to get married over his dead body." Charmaine has, unfortunately, bought into the problematic belief that black women are incomplete without a socially approved marital partner. Charmaine sees conjure as her only option, "if'n you want something bad enough that praying takes too long," because she longs to be whole, a wholeness that can only be fulfilled by a husband. As the trio of gossips proclaim: "All she needs is a good, solid man!" Charmaine fails to recognize that she was never bereft because her community will not allow it. Newsome deftly offers a racially gendered revision of the horror genre by focusing on the rich folklore of the African diaspora, specifically the practice of conjure. And it is conjure and similar tools of West African mystical agency that provide a central foundation for black women creators' transformation of the horror genre explored in this chapter.

Throughout this project, I have explored the presence of the black woman in horror—whom I earlier named Sycorax—and how her presence complicates mainstream horror theory, black feminist theory, and genre writing as a whole. The previous chapter used my critical framework—fluid fiction—to demonstrate how black women writers redefine genre literature by purposely conflating and separating genres by redefining them within an Africanized feminist context. This chapter builds upon the concept of fluid fiction—accepting that black women's creative works flow between the definitions of genre—but the women I analyze in this chapter use the flowing nature of their pieces to specifically revise and redefine the genre of horror. I insist that Sycorax is done haunting horror; by refusing to remain a specter, Sycorax chooses to incarnate—on her own black feminist terms—through the writing, music performance, and visual art of the black women creators explored throughout this chapter.

The women I discuss in this chapter share a theoretical textual purpose and vision that are grounded in the principles of natal African religions. There is precedent for the incredible influence of African cosmologies and epistemologies in black women's fiction as "storytelling becomes a significant means of revising traditional historiography," for these women are privileging the subversive art of storytelling and imbuing it with the authority too often afforded only to the historical record.[3] Scholar Venetria K. Patton insists that black women writers "tap into the power" of the ancestral wisdom of their African ancestors.[4] This wisdom informs black women writers' most foundational idea, the knowledge that the spiritual and physical worlds are incredibly intertwined and that there exists much crossover between the two cosmologies.

Black women creatives possess a unique ability to interweave African-influenced folklore with the Westernized genres of horror, fantasy, and science fiction, which coalesce into what I term folkloric horror. This chapter explores the concept of folkloric horror in four distinct sections. In the first section, I define folkloric horror and discuss how it operates as an articulation of an aesthetic theory of black women horror creators. The second section explicates how folkloric horror has a literary history in black women's writing as I explicate Gloria Naylor's *Mama Day* (1988) and Erna Brodber's *Louisiana* (1994) within the theoretical framework. I continue with a demonstration of the potential for folkloric horror to explicate contemporary black women's genre writing. I read Kiini Ibura Salaam's short story "Rosamojo" (2003) and Chesya Burke's "Chocolate Park" (2004) through the folkloric horror framework. The third section expands folkloric horror in its sonic and performative iteration as I read it through the music of Memphis Minnie and Nina Simone, whom I insist simultaneously embody the role of blueswoman and conjure women in intentionally subversive ways.

Black women are nearly invisible in the horror industry in all of its manifestations—publishing, conventions, and community—with only a few notable exceptions. Tananarive Due has become a staple in the horror industry—her works are popular and well-regarded, and she has been nominated for several Bram Stoker Awards and has been awarded the National Book Award for *The Living Blood* (2001) and an NAACP Image Award.[5] Linda Addison—a horror poet—has won numerous Bram Stoker Awards and has also become a respected editor and cheerleader for women of color writers in the horror community.[6] Yet too many black women horror writers remain unacknowledged and underappreciated in the genre's publishing and surrounding industries. A rising cohort of black women horror creators refuse to be invisible—following the advice of bell hooks, these women are teaching us how to see them and their work.[7]

The increasing visibility of black women horror writers began with an entry titled "20 Black Women in Horror Writing" on horror writer Sumiko Saulson's professional blog.[8] Saulson attempted to be exhaustive, including writers as varied as Octavia Butler, LA Banks, Pearl Cleage, N. K. Jemisin, and Nalo Hopkinson. The response to this list was overwhelming, mostly positive, but also informing Saulson of so many other black women horror writers she missed—leading to the subsequent entries, "21 More Black Women in Horror Fiction" and its follow-up, "19 More Black Women in Horror Fiction."[9] Ultimately, Saulson published an eBook titled *60 Black Women in Horror Fiction* (2014) that lists the writers along with their works and interviews, where available.[10]

The sole purpose of the website and social media presence of the collective—Graveyard Shift Sisters—is to fight against the invisibility of black women in horror. The first line of their Mission Statement demonstrates that the collective "aims to highlight and celebrate the experiences and achievements of Black women . . . in the horror (and science fiction) genre."[11] The website features a trove of blog posts analyzing black women's place in contemporary horror, horror movie reviews, and in-depth interviews with black women horror creators, with a significant emphasis on film studies. The very name of the collective acknowledges black women's poor representation: "It dawned on us that the graveyard shift itself is that undesirable time to work and be. In a society of 9 to 5 visibility and for some, normalcy, the graveyard shift is held by those willing to take the slot no one really wants, and for some, taking it with limited choices. It's a space where the invisible dwell, the marginalized." Spaces like Graveyard Shift Sisters ultimately reject the notion of invisibility and recognize the disjunctures in which black women are so often doing the necessary work to define themselves. The eschewing of the false idea of invisibility remains the focus of this chapter, for I maintain that black women have always been creating horror texts—not unlike Sycorax's essence that suffuses Prospero's island—it is the task of this chapter to privilege the multiplicities that black women writers demand of horror in creating their own creative horror aesthetic—folkloric horror.

Toward a Black Women's Horror Aesthetic

It is necessary to begin with an explication of what black women horror creators are not doing—and such a critique can be found in the oft-misplaced line of critical inquiry that reads black women's' supernatural writings as magical realism. Magical realism is "a style of literature which integrates a realist mode of writing with fantastical or marvelous events treated as perfectly ordinary occurrences . . . [which] enable the writer to critique belief, memory, and the imagination as historical forces."[12] Magical realism is also steeped in Latin American writing culture and tradition—it has since been applied to other writers of color, Salmon Rushdie and Toni Morrison. I suggest that the (even partial) application of magical realism to black women's supernatural literature is ill-conceived. Morrison herself chafes under the application of magical realism to her novels because the practice is both lazy and ahistorical, for it operates on the assumption that she is not without a literary tradition.[13] Magical realism ignores African Americans' long-standing oral and literary history of including the supernatural and the fantastical in our narratives, such as Charles Waddell Chesnutt's *The Conjure Woman* (1899) and Zora Neale Hurston's *Every Tongue Got to Confess: Negro Folk-tales from the Gulf States* (1929).

What is necessary, and what the rest of this section ponders upon, is making an argument for a black woman's aesthetic of horror. The search for a black women's horror aesthetic does not begin with this chapter. A growing number of black women horror creators and their fans are examining the ever-expanding list of texts and have subsequently initiated a discerning conversation discussing what constitutes black women's aesthetics in horror. Many authors—Jewelle Gomez, Jemiah Jefferson, and Nalo Hopkinson, to name a few—have considered the concept during individual interviews and roundtable participation. Similarly, black women in horror film—writers, directors, and actresses—have begun to outline their thoughts on a black women's horror aesthetic. Ashlee Blackwell, creator of the website/blog Graveyard Shift Sisters, posts an entry that attempts to synthesize the work of black women and horror films as she ponders: "I am curious as to why horror isn't a space where a number of Black women are exercising cinematic efforts in tackling supernatural stories that feel familiar."[14] Blackwell's entry does not provide any easy answers, as she continues to use the blog and its resources to search for answers. Blackwell's entry does lend an interesting set of questions to launch my own inquiry: "What horrors are directly related to black women? What elements, themes, aesthetic appeal would make a horror film a solid example of Black female centrality and agency?"[15] Though I work beyond the realm of film to include multiple texts, Blackwell's questions ground my contention that the folkloric horror framework articulates an aesthetic of black women horror creators.

A black women's horror aesthetic proves necessary in order to "show [the reader] how to look" at the works of authors writing through multiple identities.[16] The creators discussed in this chapter are "fashioning an aesthetic of being" through horror literature, music performance, and film, thereby making the subversive nature of their work "a force to be made and imagined."[17] Critic bell hooks argues that "we must learn to see" black aesthetics—I push her intellectual trajectory further in the application of her argument for black aesthetic theory to include black women horror writers.

Folkloric horror "critically conceptualize[s] a radical aesthetic that does not negate the powerful place of theory as both the force that sets up criteria for aesthetic judgment and as vital grounding that helps make certain work possible, particularly expressive work that is transgressive and oppositional."[18] The use of fluid fiction writing techniques specifically applied to the horror genre carves a space for the authors to interrogate oppressive structures of the Western hegemony. The women are actively writing against "the assumption that naturalism or realism [is] more accessible to a mass audience than abstraction."[19] In truth, the women are revising Nnedi Okorafor's notion of "organic fantasy" by engaging horror in using fiction to reflect greater truths of the African diasporic experience.[20] Unfortunately, the implementation of horror has previously led to the dismissal of the significance of the work of black women horror creators—a practice that becomes outdated with the construction of folkloric horror as a black women's aesthetic of horror.

Folkloric horror is a theoretical framework that attempts to fill a critical lacuna in the reading of black women horror writers. Black feminist speculative fiction critics Gwendolyn Pough and Yolanda Hood have consistently recognized the need to acknowl-edge the unique nature of horror when black women produce it.[21] There is an endeavor in the Pough and Hood piece to recognize the important relevance of horror—as well as an attempt to name it "speculative horror"—but it still falls short in incorporating the multiplicities of identity and genre that guide black women horror creators. Folkloric horror answers Hood and Pough's call for a new hybrid of speculative horror.[22]

Folkloric horror is comprised of four distinct yet interrelated facets. First, folkloric horror highlights knowledge systems grounded in the cosmologies of natal African religions such as Vodou, Obeah, and Santería. The purposeful act of predicating their fiction within a non-Western epistemology allows the writers to unceasingly sub-vert mainstream horror. Subversion continues with the respectful approach these women bring to these traditional religions—African epistemologies are centered and treated as, if not commonplace, then certainly worthy of their place of privilege within their texts.

This is markedly different from the derogatory and, dare I say it, dangerous constructions of traditional African religions in mainstream horror.[23] The second aspect of folkloric horror is its acceptance of spiritual possession as a valid ontology and valued epistemological tool. Multiple plot points of the texts analyzed in this chapter center on ancestors and loas/orishas possessing their descendants and passing on valuable knowledge in the form of divination and oral narratives. Religious scholar John S. Mbiti proclaims that, within African ontologies, "man is a forever creature, but he does not remain forever man."[24] The protagonists develop complex relationships with what Mbiti refers to as the living-dead—the newly dead that are physically dead but are often kept alive as "guardians of family affairs, traditions, ethics, and activities."[25] The blurring of the lines between humans and their living-dead ancestors, as well as the orishas and other spirits, Africanizes the subversive notion that death is not final and affords diasporic peoples a "personal and collective immortality," thus radically revising two mainstream horror tropes—the ghost and the zombie.[26] Next, folkloric horror privileges the experience of the spiritual bildungsroman, the discovery of a young woman's powerful self while under the tutelage of spiritual mentors and elders. This feature acts as a powerful modification of fantasy literature's idea of "The Journey." Patton places the elders encountered in these texts in the role of "culture bearer," for these spiritual mentors "often remind us that the future has a past and the past must not be forgotten."[27] Finally, folkloric horror builds upon the previously mentioned qualities to center itself on the realization and celebration of the black spiritual feminine to achieve a revised literary articulation of the Mambo, the Santera, and the Obeah woman. It must be noted that the multiple texts explored in this chapter manifest different gradations of these elements, as many privilege certain facets over others.

Folkloric Horror in Black Women's Literature

I have steadily alluded to the presence of horror tropes in classic black women's literature that is suffused with ghosts, curses, and psychological terror, such as Toni Morrison's *Beloved* (1987). In this section, I want to continue my earlier contention by recognizing and explicating the horror elements in Gloria Naylor's *Mama Day* and Erna Brodber's *Louisiana* through the folkloric horror framework. *Mama Day* focuses on the trials of the Day women on the small autonomous island of Willow Creek. The plot follows the original maternal ancestor/goddess of the Day family, Sapphira Wade; the contemporary heir to her supernatural powers, Miranda, or Mama Day; as well as the powers' future inheritor Ophelia, or Cocoa Day. *Louisiana* centers on the journey of Ella Townsend and her travels with the Works Progress Administration (WPA) to rural Louisiana to interview and research the stories of two best friends—Mammy and Lowly—who communicate their stories beyond the veil of death. I privilege these two texts because both are respected exemplars of black women's literature and are routinely explored in multiple iterations of black feminist literature. Both works also share spiritual and supernatural elements explored in previous analyses that vigorously evaded the unwelcome label of horror.

Mama Day and *Louisiana* both privilege epistemes that reflect traditional African religious cosmologies. The character Mama Day is a powerful conjure woman with knowledge of healing herbs and a connection with Willow Springs' ancestors. Though not as formally organized as Vodou, Santería, or Candomblé, Hoodoo (or conjure) contains a set of practices that are heavily grounded in traditional African belief systems that also incorporate syncretic elements of Christianity. Mama Day casts multiple spells throughout the novel using her extensive plant knowledge and access to ancestral communications. Her work is often benevolent in intention—she includes a fine yellow powder in Cocoa's letter to her future husband, George Andrews, to push their connection further. Mama Day also aids Bernice on multiple occasions in her quest to conceive a child—she saves Bernice's ability to reproduce by healing her from the "fertility" pills that flare her endometriosis, and she ultimately conducts a secret ceremony to impregnate her with her son. The characterizations of Mama Day, Louise, and

Anna reinforce Patton's suggestion that elders "maintain traditions and keep communities tied to their past in a way which promotes communal health."[28] Similarly, *Louisiana* privileges the less formal Hoodoo in manifesting natal African religious practices—particularly early in the novel. After Louise's death, Mama Day and Anna continue to share their stories with Ella through the gramophone. Ella's journey begins and ends with the privileging of ancestral knowledge, eventually leading her to a divine state rooted in the African.

It is the privileging of ancestral knowledge that leads to the acceptance of spiritual possession as a valid ontology and valued epistemological tool in both *Louisiana* and *Mama Day*. Mammy (Anna) and Lowly (Louise), her matriarchal ancestors, eventually possess Ella and form a trinity, or a communal "I."[29] The process of containing three women and three consciousnesses in one body is easily accepted by Ella's husband, Reuben, as well as their neighbors in the disenfranchised black community of New Orleans. The community eventually accepts her not as Ella but as Louisiana—a play on her possession as Ella embodies "Louise y Ana." The character Louisiana becomes a community leader and respected matriarch composed of the hard-won knowledge and power bestowed by her ancestors—she embodies and promotes the notion of healthy manifestations of African diasporic community. Cocoa is cursed by a neighbor, Ruby, when she is seen interacting with her lover, Junior Lee. The curse reveals Cocoa to be possessed by an evil entity manifested as tiny, clear worms that are crawling inside her body and sucking the life and sanity out of her very essence. Everyone in the Day family and the community of Willow Springs accepts the disturbing ontological presentation that is Cocoa's curse, everyone except for her rational and logical engineer husband, George. It is George's inability to accept Cocoa's cursed nature and to accept the Africanized knowledge being offered to him that highlights the elements of folkloric horror explored in *Mama Day*. George refuses to acknowledge the supernatural element causing Cocoa's sickness—even when he discovers a small clear worm on the head of his penis after having sex with his wife.

George also actively refuses to open himself to the wisdom of the African when he continuously eschews Mama Day's advice when she asks him to bring her an egg from the hen house. George is so focused on the tangible—attempting and failing to find the egg, for he is attacked by a rooster—that he is unable and unwilling to understand Miranda's request for establishing faith in that which cannot be seen. Ultimately, George dies for his inability to accept the power of the spiritual world.

Miranda's failed attempt to mentor George parallels her more successful mentorship of her granddaughter, Cocoa, as she comes into her own as the inheritor of Sapphira Wade's powers. Both Cocoa and Ella undergo a spiritual coming of age under the tutelage of their maternal ancestors, both living and living-dead. Naylor's exceptional construction of Cocoa's husband, George, and her elusive great-aunt, Miranda Day, has often left analyses of Cocoa bereft in number and scrutiny. Here, I suggest that the true purpose of the characters and aim of the plot is the spiritual preparation of Cocoa for eventually replacing Mama Day as a community matriarch and as the physical manifestation of Sapphira Wade's Africanized knowledge and healing powers. Each of Cocoa's experiences leads her to the final scene of the novel in which she is visiting George's grave remarried and a mother preparing to permanently settle in Willow Springs and to continue to learn under Mama Day in a more intense matter. The novel centers on Cocoa's spiritual development as she settles on the island of Manhattan, meets and marries George, brings him home to Willow Springs, is cursed and possessed by evil, and loses George because of his inability to let go of rationality. Each moment becomes a trial by fire in which Cocoa increases her knowledge of herself and comes to accept her place in the maternal line. It is necessary to note that the successful campaign to prepare Cocoa for her new life is achieved through the maneuverings between her living elders, Mama Day, and her living-dead ancestor, Sapphira Wade.

Ella also undergoes a spiritual bildungsroman as she slowly metamorphoses from Ella to Louisiana. Ella and her husband remain in Louisiana after Louisa's death—choosing to live in

New Orleans, a city ripe with spiritual energy. Ella's initiation begins with the voices she hears from the WPA gramophone revealing stories of Mammy's and Lowly's lived realities, travels, and even community work for Marcus Garvey. Ella eventually undergoes a physical sickness that keeps her bedridden so that she can undergo the necessary spiritual formation by being possessed by the two ancestors. The process only takes a few days, and Louisiana emerges and begins to come into her own. She begins to offer spiritual advice, ensconces herself into the working-class communities of New Orleans, converts to vegetarianism, and begins to dress in all-white.[30]

Louisiana's adoption of all-white as her dress code expresses the fourth and final aspect of folkloric horror, the realization and celebration of the black spiritual feminine as a revised literary interpretation of the Mambo, the Santera, and the Obeah woman.[31] As Louisiana develops, she begins to be associated with Marie Leveau, a famous Vodou priestess popular since the nineteenth century. Brodber is purposeful in revising Lousiana's elucidation

FIG. 9. Two Iyawos of the Lucumi faith.

of Madame Marie, for Louisiana's spirituality is read through the significance of her all-white dress. Here, Brodber borrows heavily from traditional African religious practices, specifically the process of becoming an Iyawo, the Yoruba word for "bride." In Vodou, an advanced practitioner literally marries her personal loa, hence becoming a bride. In Santeria, advanced practitioners who have received their "head" or "ori" and are chosen as priests/priestesses wear white, for they have become newly born in their relationship with their tutelary orisha.[32] Louisiana adopts the spiritual mandates of the Iyawo, who is expected to "observe a year dressed entirely in white with strict behavioral restrictions including not being out at night, not taking things from other people's hands and not cutting their hair."[33] Hence we see that in privileging the presence and journey to the black spiritual feminine, Brodber blurs the lines between the religious delineations and focuses on heightening the connection to the African that suffuses them all.

Naylor similarly blurs the denominations of the syncretic manifestations of the African religions by placing her celebratory character, Mama Day, as a conjure woman, a practitioner of the hazily defined practices of Hoodoo. Mama Day does not wear white, nor does she eat a special diet, but she is a mother to every occupant of Willow Springs. Though she does not have any biological issue, she has birthed every person on the island through midwifery. She is both a healer and a spiritual counselor, and her placement in the community is revered just as any spiritual leader. Yet similar to the Obeah women of Jamaica, Mama Day can work a root using her herbal knowledge and imbuing it with the spiritual powers found in The Other Place. It is The Other Place, the former home of Sapphira Wade in which the majority of her African-derived powers can be found, that Naylor celebrates the spiritual feminine of the black woman. The Other Place is the setting for the ceremony Bernice undergoes to conceive her son outside the natural laws of fertility as wielded by Mama Day. Mama Day also demonstrates noted aspects of the Mambo, for she possesses a magnificent talent for composing a gris-gris—a New Orleans Vodou spell—and using it against someone who has attacked her family. Mama Day invokes a gris-gris as she curses Ruby and her house, slapping a mix of herbs on the house with her open hand as she proclaims a short invocation that later causes lightning to strike Ruby's home and destroy it—with her still in it.

I have used this section to explore how horror has had a steady presence in what is considered classic black women's literature. Close readings of *Louisiana* and *Mama Day* also exposed the value in the critical framework of folkloric horror when used as a tool to examine a black women's horror aesthetic. The framework sustains both early and newer demonstrations of black women's horror fiction. The next section investigates the value of folkloric horror in reading works of contemporary black women horror writers.

Folkloric Horror in Contemporary Black Women Horror Creators

The contemporary women are paying homage even as they revise elements of folkloric horror. The stories I examine in this section, "Chocolate Park" by Chesya Burke and "Rosamojo" by Kiini Ibura Salaam, follow the black feminist literary tradition of tackling difficult subjects that affect black women's lived realities—but actively use horror and supernatural elements to highlight the ways that African spirituality offers both problems and solutions. Yet they often bring in contemporary horror tropes such as zombies and demons to adapt the more classic literatures to their own horror aesthetic. The most exciting element contemporary writers offer is the exploration of moral gray areas, for they purposely complicate the false dichotomies of good and evil.

"Chocolate Park" centers on two families living in a tenement building in the projects of the inner city and the horrific effects that drug use and poverty have on these families.[34] A family of three sisters—Sable, a young teenager of fifteen with the goal of becoming a doctor; Ebony, the middle daughter and family caretaker in her late teens with a good job at the phone company; and Coco (or Chocolate), a crack addict who has graduated to commercial sex work in exchange for money and drugs. The girls are learning to survive and cope after the death of their mother. Ebony—in particular—struggles as she fights to keep her younger sister safe and her older sister off the streets. The other family consists of Lady Black, an older black women who is both feared and respected throughout the community for her dark spiritual talents. Lady Black is also a woman in mourning, pained by the death of her son, Jacob, at the hands of the local drug dealer, Torch, and plotting vengeance.

Burke plays with multiple elements from folkloric horror—she actively celebrates the epistemological benefits of traditional African religions by constructing several intense scenes in which she rights the wrongs of the project's predators by enacting spiritual justice. Though the exact nature of her religion is not specified, Burke describes a nude Lady Black, perspiring in her small broom closet as she kneels at an alter set lit with red candles as she chants and uses the likeness of a small yellow doll beset with the discarded cigarette butt of a local pedophile, Fast Charley.[35] The reader experiences Lady Black's rapture as she dips the doll's wax penis into a container of lye and hears the screams of the sexual predator as she relishes that his flesh will continue to corrode from the penis out until there is nothing left. Again Burke is subverting folkloric horror's celebration of the divine feminine, for Lady Black lacks the inherent goodness of Brodber's Louisiana as well as the foundation of love that spurs Naylor's Mama Day.

The motives of Lady Black are dark, as she is powered by a furious anger that strips her humanity—her eyes sometimes flash red whenever she runs into predators such as Fast Charley or Torch.[36] Lady Black herself is not evil, but she is not above using evil to avenge her son's death and Sable's rape by killing Torch or protecting the young girls of the projects by destroying Fast Charley. Mama Day remains mostly benevolent and commits one act of vengeance, killing Ruby, as justice for Cocoa. Though Lady Black is a similar celebration of the black spiritual feminine, she is not at all benevolent. The very meaning of her real name, Dieula-Marie Balan, is "God is here," and demonstrates how Burke is writing against the expected goodness and generous nature of the black woman elder as spiritual leader. Though lacking benevolence, Lady

Black is still kind; she enjoys serving the community by aiding those who visit her apartment to seek spiritual counseling and justice. Burke even hints at the possibility of a spiritual mentorship between Lady Black and Sable; she even refers to Sable as her favorite Musketeer out of the pet name she has for the sisters, The Three Musketeers.

It is Lady Black that Sable runs to after being brutally gang-raped by Torch and his buddies, for her apartment is a proven safe space in which she has consistently sought refuge. Lady Black and Sable share a deep connection; Sable reminds Lady Black of her younger self, and Sable psychically informs Lady Black that she has decided to murder Coco. Sable achieves spiritual maturity through the trauma of rape and ensures her spiritual and physical survival with the blood sacrifice of her sister, Coco. Sable shoots her twice in the chest, and they bury her in Chocolate Park as an offering to the gods, ensuring their freedom from the projects forever. It is with this final element of folkloric horror—the acceptance of spiritual possession as a valid ontology and epistemological tool—that Burke has the most fun and advances contemporary modes of horror. In the final scenes, Lady Burke offers her blood and eventually her life to receive justice from the gods against Torch. The gods possess the decayed bodies of Lady Black's son (Jacob) and Coco—rendering them murderous zombies that burn him alive, just as he burned his victims.

Kiini Ibura Salaam is another writer who enjoys cavorting among the elements of the folkloric horror framework while contemplating the lived realities that black girls' experience through sexual abuse. Her short story "Rosamojo" centers on the title character, a young girl who is the middle child in a normative middle-class black family in New Orleans. The plot follows Rosamojo as she deals with situations that are far from normal—her father has begun visiting her at night, and she is terrified that her mother will discover the horror as well as her burgeoning powers to work powerful gris-gris. Again we are bereft of an exact name for the powerful African ceremonies Rosamojo ultimately performs, but Salaam's silence marks the need for naming as unnecessary to her specific tale.[37] Yet the presence of African religious traditions in the story demonstrates folkloric horror. Rosamojo grows spiritually without the guidance of an elder woman mentor; in fact, Salaam highlights just how alone she is as she lays in her bed, terrified from the assault her father has just visited upon her. In the morning, Rosa becomes obsessed with hiding her stained sheets (there are two red marks on the sheets assumed to be blood) so her mother never suspects anything untoward. She spends the entire day washing the sheets in secret, hanging them out to dry away from her neighbor's prying eyes, and finally making sure her bed is made correctly.

Rosa is so very alone, and yet she forces herself to grow in her spiritual gifts. Immediately after her daddy gets off of her, Rosa keeps a lock of his hair for the gris-gris she's planning before she even realizes it. As the cleaned wet sheets dry, Rosa enters her parents' bedroom and absconds away with her father's favorite harmonica, a newspaper he's handled that's covered in his fingerprints, and his toothpicks. Rosa carefully gathers the materials together, layering them as she places them in a bowl and alights the entire pile. It is here that Salaam revises the folkloric horror elements of spiritual possession and spiritual tutelage—Rosa experiences multiple moments of intensely advanced spiritual knowledge when performing the incantations for the spell: "As I squat, watching it burn, my lips begin to move. Words come spilling out of my mouth, spelling out a protection prayer I never knew I had in my head."[38] Rosa has a similar experience later that night as she waits for her father to come home. She grabs some of her father's cotton balls and sits on them as she begs the spirits for protection: "and those prayers start coming out of me again. This time, they come so fast, it's scary. I sit there for hours mumbling to myself, waiting for daddy to come home."[39] Rosa is both possessed by and learns from the spirits she calls to for protection. Salaam has remixed and re-visioned folkloric horror to allude to the possibility of demonic possession—a stronger horror trope rarely associated with black women's literature. Yet Rosa is not possessed by demons, but by ancestral spirits that are ubiquitous within the physical human plane.[40] Rosa is not possessed by a specifically named spirit or living-dead ancestor but by a spirit that is "depersonalized resi-due of individual human beings," or rather "withered individu-al[s]" that have joined together to manifest a great power over man found only when they gather in large numbers.[41]

Similar to Lady Black, Salaam offers us a female protagonist who commits a questionably moral act—she kills her father. The protection spell fails to work. Her father enters her room again that night, and she dumps her belongings out of the gris-gris bag around her neck and stuffs it with the cotton she has blessed along with the burnt offerings of her father's possessions leftover from the earlier incantation and replaces the bag around her neck: "I put my hand out in front of me and daddy stops short. I turn my palm up to the ceiling and imagine daddy's heart resting in my grasp. The second I feel the weight of his heart in my hand, I snap my fingers shut. Daddy gasps and bends over. I squeeze until the thing stops beating. Daddy stumbles away." The choice to kill is not without consequence—even when it can be justified—as experienced with Lady Black. The spirits do not require Rosa to pay with her life, but she is banished from her home when her mother figures out that Rosa is responsible for her father's death. Rosa must now live with her grandmother—but she is not alone in her punishment. Rosa's greatest consequence is to be haunted by the spirit of her father: "Rosa, you holdin me back . . . I need you to forgive me so I can go where I need to go." But Rosa is weary and just as alone as she was before everything happened, and she refuses to forgive her father if he can't find a way to share the truth with her mother. The story ends as Rosa declares herself a child unwilling to deal with grown-up concerns, and here Salaam subverts the celebra-tion of the spiritual feminine as a knowledgeable priestess of the Divine. Rosa is knowledgeable, powerful, and enlightened, but she has fought the entire story for the right to remain a little girl.

Folkloric Horror in Black Women's Music

The horror themes found in black women's writing are not unfa-miliar to those acquainted with their other cultural productions.

Music has long been a tool of conjure—from the beat of the djembe drum to call upon the loas to the gentle melodies of "Bringing in the Sheaves" as worshippers welcome the Holy Spirit into their midst. Music possesses the ability to bring the supernatural to an otherwise ordinary space. Blues music—a secularized revision of gospel—exists within the mythology of guitar player Robert Johnson, who allegedly sold his soul to Satan at a Mississippi crossroad to gain untold talent.[42] Johnson's story is the most popular example of magic, place, and music working together to conjure power, but many others abound—particularly in the musical performances and personas of blues singers Memphis Minnie and Nina Simone. The idea of place is consistently privileged when discussing conjure, and black women exist at the ultimate crossroad—the intersection of race and gender. I insist that the aforementioned women are using the concept of the blueswoman to expand folkloric horror within a musical context to conjure the supernatural out of the deceptively ordinary. Sonic folkloric horror consists of three characteristics—it is based in the intentional, simultaneous occupation of the role of the blueswoman and the conjure woman; this simultaneity is based in traditional West African religious practices; and, most important, these black women musicians possess the ability to conjure through their musical performances.

Conjure, often associated with the Hoodoo, is a set of practices associated with faith and healing but not with one specific religion. In her monograph *Black Magic: Religion and the African American Conjuring Tradition* (2006), scholar Yvonne P. Chireau defines conjure as "a magical tradition in which spiritual power is invoked for various purposes, such as healing, protection, and self defense."[43] Conjure is mainly practiced by black Americans descended from Africans enslaved in the United States. Chireau and other scholars, such as Trudier Harris have long associated conjure with folklore, terming it a "set of folk beliefs common to slaves" and yet distinct from the formalities of "black church rituals."[44] Scholar Kameelah L. Martin defines conjure as spirit work: "I mean to suggest an intimacy with both the healing and harming ritual practices of African-derived religious practices that evolved in the New World. . . . [It] also involves, as the term suggests, communication with supernatural entities that in some cultures may be referred to as ghosts, ha'ints, specters, or apparitions but across the African diaspora are known as the Ancestors, loa, orisha, or simply Spirit."[45] Martin, like many other scholars, also connects the practice of conjure to African American folklore through the figure of the conjure woman.

The conjure woman is a figure of power whose presence suffuses the oral narratives of African American folklore and its cultural products. She is a woman of power who possesses the knowledge of medicinal herbs, midwifery, magic, and even counseling through a specific connection to the spirit realm. The conjure woman is first introduced into the literary consciousness by the author Charles W. Chesnutt in his collection of stories titled *The Conjure Woman* (1899). The book's structure is a literary reflection of the oral folklore passed through the generations of African descendants in the United States.[46] Martin furthers Harris's intimation of the conjure woman as a literary archetype throughout her project, but her most interesting claim is her suggestion that the conjure woman attains the status of folk hero: "The conjure woman . . . [has] a history that has roots in black folks['] culture. The connection of the conjure woman to a real, tangible cultural expression raises her to the status of a revered icon, a standing of which neither the mammy nor the tragic mulatoo can boast. As such, the conjure woman's prominence in African American literature reflects the genealogy of a folk hero who actually lived among the people."[47]

Though folk heroes, conjure women were real people held in both esteem and disdain in African American communities throughout the United States. Conjure women occupied an interstitial position in society that reflected the intersectional role they played as midwife, herbalist, fortuneteller, relationship counselor, and spiritual adviser. The power of foresight was both a gift and a burden, marking conjure women as outcasts, however revered they may have been. Chireau determines conjure women as "socially marginalized" women who were depicted as "outsiders, inhabitants of the fringes, dwelling within a cultural demimonde."[48] I contend that the marginalized status of the conjure woman mirrors the simultaneously celebrated and excluded sociocultural status of the legendary blueswoman. In my quest to explore how black women performers manifest folkloric horror through the intentionally simultaneous play between the conjure woman and the blueswoman, I find it necessary to discuss the already established relationship between the blues and conjure.

Lady Sings the Blues

The historical connection between the blues and conjure stems from the blues' status as a musical form derived from the Negro spirituals of the enslaved. Post-emancipation, the spiritual developed into the more formalized gospel music, which converged with the aspirational respectability of the traditional Black Church.[49] The blues are comprised of the viscera that remains— that which did not survive the spiritual's metamorphosis into the more rigid and appropriate boundaries of gospel music. Angela Y. Davis insists that in the cosmology of enslaved Africans, the secular and the sacred were far more intertwined: "the sacred universe was virtually all-embracing" and refused to account for the concept of such "polar opposites" the postemancipatory black community attempted to revise.[50] Blues ideals incorporated a focus on the individual—allowing folks to privilege the desires of one above the many. Blues ideals focused on the corporeal, acknowledging the importance of the needs of the flesh, the need to dance, to make love, to drink, and to *feel*.

Davis contends that the blues "displace[d] sacred music in the everyday lives of black people," referring to the songs as "secular spirituals," but I want to push back at this contention.[51] I assert that the blues did not displace the sacred; the blues were simply another form of interacting with the sacred, fulfilling the intrinsic lack of the complex importance of the body found in the "respectable" traditional Black Church. The sacrosanct nature of the blues can be seen in its manifestation and sociocultural importance, which intertwines with its spiritual significance. Chireau refers to the blues as "African American theodocity." While insisting that both the "blues *and* spirituals are a form of worship and celebration," she furthers her argument by referring to blues artists as "musical ministers."[52] My contentions build upon Chireau's naming the relationship between the blues and African American spirituality as a "paradigm of kinship."[53]

The sacramental nature of the blues exists because of the immense power the blues initiate in the intimacy between the musician and the audience. I insist that this power is perpetuated through conjure, another manifestation of the sacred eschewed by mainstream African American Christian practice. I further posit that both the blues and conjure simultaneously subvert the false binaries of institutionalized black Christianity. Martin insists that there is "a symbiotic relationship between conjure and blues music that originated in postemancipation cultural production."[54] Blues music contains "songs of power" and often acted as a "vessel through which conjure reached a broad audience."[55] Chireau, Martin, and Davis use their projects for in-depth examinations of the presence of conjure in blues music. Chireau reads blues songs for explicit ingredients for conjure spells such as Lizzie Miles's *Shootin' Star Blues* (1928), even as Davis connects the themes of conjure in the lyrics and titles of blues songs with specific West African cultural practices.[56] Martin's exploration of conjure and the blues goes even further, as she discusses specific conjurers of the day immortalized in song and studies how themes of conjure suffused blues music: "Blues music in many ways immortalizes not only conjure practice but also the Hoodoo doctors and conjure women who were famously recognized for their power."[57] The rest of this chapter examines what most piques my critical interest while simultaneously filling a gap in the scholarship, the symbiotic relationship between the blueswoman and the conjure woman.

Existing at the Crossroads of Blueswoman and Conjure Woman

Farah Jasmine Griffin posits that the voice of the black woman has the power to cast spells.[58] It is here I want to explore the nuances of how certain black women performers simultaneously draw upon and embody the blueswoman and the conjure woman, thus manifesting folkloric horror. Such a feat is not as far-fetched as it seems. The previous section discussed the well-established kinship between the blues and conjure; it is only a small step to examining the interweaving of these traditions by black women entertainers. Martin intimates: "conjure and the blues share a more reciprocal relationship, one extending a hand to help the other. Blues music is one vessel through which conjure has reached a broad audience," and blueswoman purposely "incorporated conjure sensibilities" to became popular ambassadors of the black woman–centered belief. In truth, the blueswoman and the conjure woman occupy a similarly complex social status within the African American community. Both sets of women were communal outcasts with protofeminist ideologies who also privileged communal healing.

Blueswomen and conjure women rejected the values of the mainstream African American culture and beliefs. These women existed on the margins of society because they were often associated with practices outside the morays of the traditional Black Church—a prominent fixture in the larger community. Conjure women, though the majority of their clients were regular church attendees, operated outside of what many considered Christian grace. Their belief in forces connecting back to traditional West African religious practices forced them outside of the cultural milieu. Likewise, blueswomen were considered immoral and dangerous because of their open celebration of excess and bodily pleasures—sexuality was a prominent theme in blues music.[59] Other themes included "advice to other women; alcohol; betrayal or abandonment; broken or failed love affairs; death; departure; dilemma of staying with a man or returning to family; disease and afflictions; erotica; hell; homosexuality; infidelity; injustice; jail and serving time; loss of lover; love; men; mistreatment; murder; other woman; poverty; promiscuity; sadness; sex; suicide; supernatural; trains; traveling; unfaithfulness; vengeance; weariness, depression, and disillusionment; weight loss."[60] Davis further highlights how none of these themes included "children, domestic life, husband,

and marriage."[61] The noted lack of fit blueswomen displayed with regard to the respectable black woman gives fertile reasoning for their status as social outcasts.

The conjure woman and the blueswoman showed an agency centered in early black feminist beliefs and practices. The conjure woman trafficked in the powers associated with the black feminine. The prominent position as conjurer was gender neutral, open to folks across the gender spectrum. The marginalized status of the conjure woman also offered economic freedom, allowing "some practitioners to accumulate material wealth from their professions."[62] This was in direct opposition to the patriarchal framework of the African American church in which men were in leadership positions and were often given economic and sociocultural freedom through the economic sacrifice of black women. Conjure women also trafficked in spells or gris-gris that privileged the essence of womanhood. A popular remedy for a straying lover is to feed him a meal with a red sauce that hides the menstrual blood the woman has introduced to the meal. Davis remains fascinated by the "hints of feminist attitudes" that suffuse the performances of blueswomen as she demonstrates their participation in the construction of oral feminist traditions. Blueswomen could be economic powerhouses, at times experiencing a financial independence so often denied postemancipatory black women. But the highlight of the blueswoman's black feminist tradition remains her sexual freedom. These women eschewed marriage and husbands and reveled in bragging about the prowess of their many lovers, some of whom were female. Blueswomen also displayed a protofeminist independence of spirit by living life in the fast lane: "All of them women who'd sing the blues would curse, be drunk, just sit up and talk a lot of shit, man. What foul language!"[63]

The final theme that draws both blueswomen and conjure women together is their belief and participation in the healing powers of their gifts. There exists more clarity in how conjure women were often read as healers "who viewed healing as a sacred duty."[64] Some were midwives and were often more affordable options to medical doctors for minor ailments given their talent for herbs and tonics. Conjure women were also spiritual counselors, providing mental and emotional healing to their customers as well. Martin connects conjure itself as a cure for the condition of the blues. Blueswomen were healers who focused "on the fixing of relationships gone awry and the resolution of oppressive romantic entanglements."[65] Blueswomen would often be termed as "preachin' the blues," as their sermons on love—of the self as well as others—demonstrated the healing potential in connecting "spiritual and sexual joy."[66] Ultimately, blueswomen privileged the psychological and spiritual wellness of their audience by expelling their blues by naming it, singing it, and taking away its power.

Sonic Folkloric Horror in Black Women's Musical Performance

I use the language of Daphne Brooks to discuss the theoretically revolutionary and politically savvy ways in which these black women performed sonic folkloric horror by "conflat[ing] and pervert[ing] the boundaries of" the blueswoman and the conjure woman. Their simultaneous embodiment of the blueswoman and the conjure woman "translat[es] alienation into [a] self-actualizing performance" and ultimately "revis[es] the black cultural imaginary."[67] Memphis Minnie and Nina Simone interweave their voice and their instrument to expand the possibilities of previously limited constructions of black femininity. These women possess a remarkable talent for remixing and revising their "condition of social, political, and cultural alterity" to manifest sonic folkloric horror. The musical manifestation of folkloric horror contains varying degrees of the simultaneous embodiment of the blueswoman and the conjure woman. This embodiment occurs in musical performances that are marked by one or more specific acts of conjuring a racially gendered and defined performance self-articulation through the use of their voice accompanied by instrumentation conducted by the performer. Memphis Minnie conjures with her guitar, and Nina Simone conjures with her piano.

Memphis Minnie predates Robert Johnson, as she survived the Great Depression as a musician and went on to record music over a thirty-year span of the twentieth century.[68] Minnie was a pioneer who occupied the liminal space between the sophisticated women of the classic blues era and the unsophisticated men of the latter country blues era.[69] The majority of previous scholarship on blueswomen has focused on blues singers and not Minnie, known for her prowess with her guitar and her ability to "play like a man."[70] An analysis of Minnie's prolific music writing and performance career spanning three decades proves her no less a blueswoman. The majority of the songs she performed, such as "Black Cat Blues," "Crazy Crying Blues," and "In My Girlish Days," were written and composed by Minnie herself.[71] Minnie also assumed the protofeminist, independent, and fast-paced lifestyle of a blueswoman: "Yeah Minnie shot craps like a man, playing those cards, man, raising all kinds of hell."[72] Yet it was in her musical performance that Memphis Minnie would overlay the persona of conjure woman to intersect with her reality as a blueswoman.

In her performance of "Hoodoo Lady" Memphis Minnie uses her guitar to conjure a revision of the black cultural imaginary that highlights her otherness and otherworldly qualities. "Hoodoo Lady" is a song in which Minnie masterfully flows from first to third person throughout the lyrics and guitar riffs as easily as she oscillates in the role of blueswoman and conjure woman (see Appendix). When singing the verses, Minnie is speaking to the Hoodoo lady in the third person, but when speaking and playing the guitar riffs throughout, Minnie is embodying the Hoodoo lady as conjure woman. As previously established, a Hoodoo lady is a woman of power who commands respect. Minnie and her intended audience are well aware of the specialized status of a Hoodoo woman, and she intentionally blurs notions of power as well as the lines between the Self and the Other. Minnie is clear that she considers herself both/and while eschewing the false binary of either/or.

The song itself is a meditation on power as seen through the framework of conjure while demonstrating Minnie's lyrical dexterity. In the first verse, Minnie is respectful in speaking to the Hoodoo lady, asking "how do you do?" as she acknowledges the breadth of her conjuring abilities, "They tell me you take a boot and turn it into a brand new shoe." Minnie also possesses a startling clarity in just exactly what a danger the Hoodoo lady presents to her as she wails: "Don't put that thing on me/'Cause I'm going back to Tennessee." It is never clear just what that "thing" is—but Minnie's knowledgeable audience is aware that it infers a special sort of conjuring that doesn't result in anything good or pleasurable. Though the phrase "Don't put that thing on me/'Cause I'm going back to Tennessee" occurs in each verse of the song, here it is a beseeching request. I suggest that it changes in meaning in each of the three stanza movements, gaining agency and power throughout as Minnie conjures in the guitar riffs throughout the song. In the second stanza—still the first of three song movements—Minnie pleads her case: "I'm sitting here, broke, and I ain't got a dime" but again only after acknowledging the godlike powers of the Hoodoo lady, "you can turn water to wine." Her request, though still polite, is no longer beseeching: "You ought to put something in these dukes of mine."

It is in the guitar riffs that power imbalances shift. Minnie is specifically using her specialized strumming techniques as an empowering act of conjure and self-articulation. Bluesman Willie Moore said that Minnie "could make a guitar talk."[73] Minnie was known for her skill at "Spanish tuning," for "though fingerpicking, she plays with the speed and finesse of a flatpicker."[74] It is necessary to note that Minnie's deft guitar playing builds upon her aforementioned verbal agility. She introduces her guitar solo with the sly aside: "Boy you better watch it because she's tricky." The "she" is referring to Minnie herself, and the tricks she possesses include the ability to conjure power and cast spells with her nimble fingers. Scholar Gabriel Solis reads these particular guitar solos as a palimpsest.[75] Langston Hughes described the rhythm of her guitar as being older than her "most remote ancestor.[76] Both recognize the influence of the West African conjuring tradition in Minnie's guitar solos. Minnie is showing off while gaining agency and the confidence to confront the Hoodoo lady as an equal and demand the use of her powers.

In the second movement of the song, just after the first guitar riff and in the third and fourth stanzas, Memphis Minnie becomes brash in her (now) demands of the Hoodoo lady. There is no longer an acknowledgment of the breadth of her powers to assuage her ego, for Minnie's own sense of self has grown. Minnie now cuts to the quick in her demands: "I want you to unlock my door." Minnie's confidence in her own conjuring abilities has grown so much that she is ordering this powerful lady around with no adherence to respectful compliance. The fourth stanza begins with "Now look-a here, Hoodoo lady" and glides right into her most fervent and specific demand yet: "Bring my man back home but don't let him stay all night." The gall of this request cannot be overstated. Minnie wants the Hoodoo lady to find her man, bring him to her, stick around until after he has serviced Minnie as she sees fit, and *then* to get rid of him! Minnie slides into another guitar solo/conjuring session before moving into the third and final movement of the song.

The final stanza begins "Why look-a here, Hoodoo lady" as Minnie insists that she and the Hoodoo lady are now at the very least equals in conjuring power and community standing: "I'm your friend" as she orders her to "come back again." The double-talk and signifying are remarkable and only possible through the acts of conjuring stirred by Minnie's finesse with the guitar. The last few lines, though a final repetition of the lines found in each stanza throughout the song, have developed in meaning. What was once a beseeching request has become an admonishment, even a dare in its subversive meaning. "Don't put that thing on me" has changed to possess a secondary meaning of "Don't [you dare] put that thing on me/'Cause I'm going back to Tennessee." Her final words are "Boys, I'm scared of her" but the smirk in her voice demonstrates the reality that Minnie is anything but scared of the Hoodoo lady, and perhaps suggests that it is the Hoodoo lady who should be afraid of Minnie and her guitar. Memphis Minnie's verbal acuity builds upon her guitar acumen as the two expressive manifestations interlock and magnify her conjuring power. Ultimately, Memphis Minnie's "Hoodoo Lady" is an impressive demonstration of conjure's potential for self-articulation in a powerful rebuttal of her supposed marginalized status.

Nina Simone Casts a Spell

In a description of Nina Simone's 1964 Carnegie Hall performance of the classic aria "Pirate Jenney," scholar Daphne Brooks posits that Simone's performance "creates a productive access that obfuscates the putative transparency of the black female singer."[77] Simone is a performer who defies singularity in the reading of her work; it is necessary to wrangle with the complexities of her performances—her intentional voice inflections and modulations and the intensity—or lack thereof—of her piano chord choices. But unlike Memphis Minnie, we also have the benefit of video recordings of her live performances and can therefore layer her sartorial choices and facial expressions. Audiovisual equipment allows us to experience how Simone performed with her entire being; scholar Danielle Heard denotes Simone a "performance artist" and demands we "consider her theatricality in addition to her musicianship and celebrity."[78] I am most interested in reading Simone's conjuration of a politics of obfuscation, disruption, and agitation through her simultaneity of embodying the blueswoman and the conjure woman in her 1965 live European cover of Jalacy Hawkins's "I'll Put a Spell On You" (1956).

There is no dispute in Simone's standing as a blueswoman, though the title is one of many she can rightfully claim. Nina Simone was a classically trained pianist who was proficient in classical music, jazz, and the blues. Simone devotes an entire 1967 album, *Nina Simone Sings the Blues*, to exploring her love and admiration for the blues. It contains one of her biggest hits, "I Want a Little Sugar in My Bowl," a revision of blueswoman Bessie Smith's "Need a Little Sugar in My Bowl" (1931).[79] Apart from singing the blues, Simone also lived the privileged but marginalized life of the earlier blueswoman. Her music afforded her economic freedom, travel, and uninhibited creative and political expression, as seen in a short interview clip in which Simone proclaims that she would have chosen to be a "killer" in the fight for black civil rights and laments that all she has is her music.[80] Her music also marginalized her as an artist, for she paid dearly for privileging music and performances that centered on black liberation. Additionally, Simone's identity as a blueswoman failed to protect her from the harsh realities of black womanhood, as she was a victim of both domestic violence and untreated mental illness.[81]

Nina Simone's recorded version of "I'll Put a Spell On You" is a muted realization of Hawkins's (in)famously wild composition.[82] Gabriel Solis describes that the producers of the album version wanted the song to be sexy and sultry, features that certainly come through. The album version is narrowly confined to a reading that centers a wronged woman threatening her unfaithful male lover—she refers to him in her ad-libs with the affectation "Daddy."

In her 1965 live performance of "I'll Put a Spell On You" Simone slips into the role of conjure woman as a directly subversive counter to the recorded album version of the very same song.[83] The sultry purr from the album is gone. The performance begins with strong, sure chords that are clearly building toward a coming crescendo. The introductory chords demand the audience's patience, for they continue almost twenty seconds of an anticipatory viewing of Simone's face. Simone refuses to make direct eye contact throughout the performance. She looks down but not at her fingers moving across the keys. She looks away but never at the camera or at any other person in her live viewing audience. She exhibits control and power by refusing everyone her gaze. Simone breaks the tension with the lowly growled proclamation: "I'll Put a Spell on You." Heard insists that Simone's "ugly growl" is intentional and layered in its application: "The [growl] . . . invokes the black feminist impulse of the blues to publicly state one's pain and anger . . . while the [ugly] resonates with the shock factor of free jazz's sonic experimentation and its sounding of black nationalist rage."[84] Simone's disruptive performance denies peace and complacency to the audience.

The depth and variance of Simone's voice affectations, coupled with the intricacies of her piano play, transcend the words of the song. "I'll Put a Spell On You" is no longer a threat. Simone's manifestation of sonic folkloric horror—the spell is literally being conjured in the performance. We must heed the words of Heard in taking the whole of Simone's presence into the reading; she is dressed in then contemporary West African fashion in what appears to be a dress and, most important, a relaxed gele—a Yoruban head wrap. Thus, Simone's fashion choices link her to the West African influence in her effort to conjure onstage. It is also necessary to continuously note Simone's visage throughout the performance. Her face is relaxed yet not open. There is no smile to welcome her audience into her world, into her performance. Simone's visage is not only serious, it is focused, for a conjure woman needs the utmost concentration in working a spell. At different moments disgust, commitment, and even frustration flash across Simone's face, as she is hard at work and devoted to seeing this particular task through to fruition. Here, there is a marked difference between a blueswoman singing about conjure—as seen in Ma' Rainey's "Louisiana Hoodoo Blues"—and a blueswoman who is simultaneously a conjure woman, as seen in Simone's live performance.

Conclusion
Sycorax's Power of Revision
Reconstructing Black Women's Counternarratives

> You know who the real tempest is, don't you?
> The real storm? Is our mother Sycorax.
> —Nalo Hopkinson's "Shift"

> We want to be our own monsters.
> —Walidah Imarisha

The 2016 release of Beyoncé's audiovisual album *Lemonade* heightens the need for the development of a black women's horror aesthetic. The visuals are suffused with the presence of Santeria's orishas, Vodou's loas, and West African monstrous goddesses such as Mami Wata. The chapter "Anger" features the words of poet Warsan Shire being read by Beyoncé over the black and white visuals featuring a circle of black women dressed in white and writhing in the manner of one large, amorphous being. The audiovisual construction focuses on the problematic indistinguishability of one black woman from another by those who render them invisible and/or inconsequential.

Though the stanza I am most interested in focuses on the infidelity of the Beyoncé character's lover, it alludes to the larger intracommunal implications of failing to see black women as

FIG. 10. Beyoncé, *Lemonade* (2016).

individuals. Beyoncé reads: "If this what you truly want. I can wear her skin . . . over mine." This interlude is easily misread as an act of violence against the other woman, forcing her to pay the adulterous price for her husband's straying of affection. In a blogpost titled "Can Beyoncé Wear Another Woman's Skin and Still Be a Feminist Icon?" writer and novelist Malaka Grant accuses Beyoncé of advocating for violence against women, making her no better than the many male artists who have made millions off of the literal blood of women. Grant ultimately declares that Beyoncé's relationship with the other woman "is out of step."[1] Grant's reading is understandable but also symptomatic of reading black women's creative texts without the consideration of horror frameworks.

A consideration of horror frameworks and folklore of the African diaspora would immediately bring in a discussion of the Boo Hag.[2] The Boo Hag is a monster from Gullah folklore that features a skinless woman who borrows the skin of others until she has absorbed their entire essence.[3] Often misappropriated as a revision of the European vampire, the Boo Hag slips into one's bedroom each night until a person has expired. The Boo Hag can be easily distracted by posting a straw broom by one's bed. The Hag is compelled to count each piece of straw until the sun comes up and destroys her at dawn. The compulsion to wear another's skin, to use "her hands as gloves," becomes a creative way in which the Beyoncé character expresses her anxiety at being replaceable and indistinguishable from any other woman her lover encounters. Hence, Beyoncé uses the grotesque and the terrifying to ultimately alleviate her fears—a coping mechanism denied black women for far too long.

This text began as a search and rescue mission for Sycorax— but in truth this volume only reveals how she saves herself. Time and again Sycorax is misread as a tool of destruction, the misreading occurs in only reading one part of her destiny. Sycorax is also a powerful tool of reconstruction in particularly subversive frameworks. The first two chapters of the project analyzed how Sycorax has been consistently ignored—by both mainstream horror and black feminist theoretical frameworks. It proved easy to eschew such a mysterious and volatile concept as black women horror creators worry the lines of the already marginalized areas of inquiry, horror studies, and black feminist theory. These particular areas of study were blind to the reconstructive and revolutionary potential embodied in Sycorax. The final two chapters of this text explored those qualities in the articulation and develop of fluid fiction—a more apt term for the complexities found in black women's genre writing. Sycorax's most seditious delineation—with regard to Western hegemonic structures—solidifies in the fourth chapter's enunciation of folkloric horror, a critical framework that highlights the authority black women take to articulate intersections of African ontologies and epistemologies as well as gender, culture, and the supernatural. The creators analyzed in that fourth chapter model the character Sycorax's ability to proclaim authority and present it in such a way that directly contradicts white, male, Christian hegemonies. Finally, it is necessary to note that Sycorax herself exists beyond the boundary of death—in fact, it is as a spiritual ancestor that she becomes more powerful. Her ability to move beyond the physical limits of her earthly body even as she strengthens her influence over the mortal world emphasizes her position as a highly favored literary ancestor for black women horror creators—even amid her heretofore limited construction as a tertiary and marginalized character in Shakespeare's text. My work here has displayed Sycorax's uncanny ability to break out of her limited constituency through traditional African ontologies. Sycorax exemplifies Bonnie Berthold's insistence that the dead are not dead—she continues to live on.

Faced with a Sycorax that refuses to stay dead, this conclusion explores the complexities of how black women horror writers offer tribute. The continuing celebration of the horror genre through a black feminist framework is only the beginning. Future endeavors must further her presence while minimizing her absence in the absent presence in which she was trapped with such constrictive characterizations. Black women horror creators must support Sycorax's continued growth as an epistemological tool of establishing counternarratives. Nalo Hopkinson, an author whose work I explored in the third chapter of this book, provides a model for incorporating, pushing, and revising Sycorax in her latest short story, "Shift."[4]

The story centers on the complex relationships between Sycorax; her son, Caliban; and her daughter, Ariel. It is told in a first-person narrative form, with Ariel and Caliban alternating in moving the story forward.

Hopkinson keeps the trope of Sycorax being a woman of African descent, but she complicates it by making her characterization a North African woman—specifically modeling her on the well-established Lebanese communities that exist on the island of Jamaica. Similarly, Sycorax is grounded in horror dynamics; she haunts Caliban and remains a sorceress filled with infinite powers, "She's coming. Sycorax is coming for you. . . . Oh, there will be so much fun when she has you again!" Sycorax begins as a ghostly presence, a haint even as she slowly begins to incarnate throughout the story culminating in her magnanimous appearance four pages from the end of the story. Sycorax's absent presence in the lives of her children hearkens back to her problematic status in *The Tempest*, yet Hopkinson subverts Shakespeare by giving her both voice and embodiment. Hopkinson also pointedly initiates Sycorax's incarnation as Mami Wata, an African water deity that established the basic myths surrounding mermaids, including the water orishas Yemaja and Oshun, and is still an object of worship for many traditional African religions, most especially Vodoun.[5] Hopkinson continues to push Sycorax's African boundaries as she demands that her children refer to her as Scylla, or Charybdis incorporates European concepts of female water deities.[6] And yet both are subsumed under Hopkinson's reading of Sycorax as Mami Watu. She is Charybdis, the powerful whirlpool; Mami Wata, a beloved deity; and Scylla, the feminized monster that threatens to consume men on their life journey. Sycorax comes to embody water, which exists everywhere—but most especially, she is tempestuous water, rapidly moving with unpredictable purpose: "She has wrapped an ocean wave about her like a shawl. . . . Her writing hair foams white over her shoulders. . . . The tsunami of Sycorax's hips overflows her watery seat. Her myriad split tails are flicking. . . . With one of them, she scratches around her navel."[7] Yet even as Sycorax has been demonized and discarded, her appearance at the end of the story is not simply to scold her children—"Ariel, Caliban: stop that squabbling or I'll bind you both up in a split tree forever"—but to also reveal the love she bestows upon her children and her weariness at rescuing them from their messy and wanton lives: "Running home to Mama, leaving me with the mess he's [Caliban] made. . . . I'm getting too old to play surrogate mother to your spawn. . . . Grannie gets to do the honours. He has brought me frog children and dog children, baby mack daddies and crack babies. Brings his offspring to me, and then runs away again. And I'm getting tired of it . . . and I'm more than tired of his sister's tale tattling."[8] Sycorax is a creature of power who is incarnated and given voice—but even then, her anger, her maelstrom, all derives from a place of love. She wants more and better for her children— for them to grow up and beyond where they are in need of her constant surveillance and approval: "I want you to stop pestering your brother," she demands of Ariel.[9] What is there in the silence is that Sycorax wants her daughter to grow beyond petty sibling rivalry to develop a life filled with loves of her own. She commands of Caliban while pointing a tentacle in his direction, "you need to stop bringing me the fallouts from your sorry love life."[10] Sycorax is silently demanding that her beloved son mature and cease his failed attempts at finding himself between every pair of cream-colored thighs he encounters. Hopkinson succeeds in complicating Sycorax showing her growth in complexity as she expands the number of facets readers are welcome to read in her characterization of such a historically fearsome character.

Contemporary black women horror creators continue to actively revise both horror and black feminist literature in ways that literary criticism has failed to acknowledge. Increasing the breadth of works available can only aid in the further development of a black women's horror aesthetic that challenges staid theories and rewrites static genres. The work must continue with the creating a database of annotated bibliographic information and supporting the frameworks that increase the number and quality of horror texts written by black women, strengthening the power and complexity of Sycorax's presence in literature, music, film, and criticism.

Appendix
Creative Work Summary

28 Days Later (2002) is a science fiction horror film directed by Danny Boyle and written by Alex Garland. It stars Cillian Murphy as Jim, Naomie Harris as Selena, Brenda Gleeson as Frank, Megan Burns as Hannah, and Christopher Eccleston as Major West. The characters navigate a postapocalyptic, quarantined Britain four weeks after a deadly viral outbreak that makes humans enraged, violent, and zombielike. Random survivors Jim, Selena, Frank, and Hannah band together searching for safety. Frank is infected, but the remaining group is "rescued" by soldiers under the command of Major West. Major West has decided that the solution to the situation is to wait out the infection and, meanwhile, rape women in order to repopulate the world. The group escapes, but Jim is injured. The film cuts to twenty-eight days after their escape, showing the characters on the mend and attempting to make contact with Finnish jets flying overhead.

2001: A Space Odyssey (1968) is a science fiction horror film directed by Stanley Kubrick and written by Stanley Kubrick and Arthur C. Clarke. It stars Keir Dullea as Dr. Dave Bowman, Gary Lockwood as Dr. Frank Poole, and William Sylvester as Dr. Heywood R. Floyd. A monolith is discovered on the moon emitting a radio signal aimed at Jupiter. A secretive Jupiter mission is devised, headed by Dr. Bowman and Dr. Poole and accompanied by a few other scientists and HAL 9000, the ship's sentient computer.

HAL is thought to be "incapable of error," but astronauts begin to doubt this and plan to unplug him. HAL knows about their plan and preemptively lashes out, killing all except Dr. Bowman. Dr. Bowman defeats HAL and continues to Jupiter, where he encounters another monolith and experiences bizarre space/time marvels, which Kubrick and Clarke left open-ended for a variety of interpretations.

Abby (1974) is a Blaxploitation horror film directed by William Girdler and written by William Girdler and Gordon Cornell Layne. It stars Carol Speed as Abby, a marriage counselor; William Marshall as Dr. Williams, a professor of archaeology; and Terry Carter as Detective Emmet, Dr. William's son and Abby's husband. On an expedition in Africa, Dr. Williams releases a Nigerian spirit of sexuality (possibly Eshu, although this point is left ambiguous), which then possesses Abby. Abby must undergo a Yoruba exorcism in order to be free of the spirit.

Tananarive Due's African Immortals series includes four titles: *My Soul to Keep* (1998), *The Living Blood* (2002), *Blood Colony* (2008), and *My Soul to Take* (2011). In Due's own words, "The series follows the lives of mortals and immortals who have contact with Living Blood that can heal any ailment almost instantly, examining issues of life, loss, and mortality." *My Soul to Keep* opens the series, with Jessica and David, a couple very much in love but racked with grief when Jessica's family and friends begin meeting violent and sudden ends. David reveals that he is from an Ethiopian sect who, 400 years ago, made a pact to become immortal; this secret is one that they are willing to protect at all cost. Jessica must make impossible choices for herself, her daughters, and her husband. Four years later, in *The Living Blood*, Jessica is still reeling from the death of her husband and first daughter; but she must now protect her second daughter, Fana, from her own fate, destined by her father's legacy and the living blood that instills her with supernatural powers. *Blood Colony* continues Fana's story, as she uses her powers to help peddle Glow, a derivative of immortal blood that heals all ailments, and battle those who attempt to use her to fulfill an ancient prophecy. *My Soul to Take* is the final installment of Fana's story, in which she is entangled in a battle of love, duty, and desires. This last novel in the series also brings in characters from Due's *Joplin's Ghost*.

An American Werewolf in London (1981) is a comedy horror film written and directed by John Landis and starring David Naughton as David Kessler, Jenny Agutter as Nurse Alex Price, and Griffin Dunne as Jack Goodman. David and Jack are two American college students backpacking through the English countryside late one night, despite being warned by locals not to do so, when they are attacked by a werewolf. Jack is killed, and David is injured and taken to London, where he suffers hallucinations of his dead friend. He and Nurse Alex develop a crush on each other, but their tryst is interrupted by frequent visitations of dead Jack, pleading for David to take his own life before the full moon. The full moon rises, and David turns into a werewolf, going on a rampage through London. He is eventually killed by the police, but only after a tearful plea from Alex fails to compose him.

Jay Anson's novel *The Amityville Horror* (1977) claims to be a true story, although this claim has caused controversy. What is verifiable is that on November 13, 1974, at the 112 Ocean Avenue residence in Amityville, Long Island, New York, Ronald DeFeo Jr. shot and killed his wife and five children. In December of the following year, the Lutz family move into the Dutch Colonial house with the now iconic gambrel roof, but they only remain for twenty-eight days. The Lutzes knew about the murders, so they ask Father Mancuso to bless the house. While administering holy water and reciting the blessing, Father Mancuso hears a male voice telling him to "get out." Later on the phone, he tries to warn the Lutzes to stay out of the second-floor bedroom, but his warning is cut short from static on the line. What is not verifiable is what the Lutz family experienced the following month. Various disturbing phenomena occur until mid-January, when they abruptly leave, unable to handle the strange and often vindictive forces at work. Sequels and films have been based off of their account.

Angel (1999–2004) is a television show spinoff of the *Buffy the Vampire Slayer* series created by Joss Whedon and David Greenwalt. It stars David Boreanaz as Angel and Charisma Carpenter as Cordelia. The show follows the conflicted character Angel (from *Buffy the Vampire Slayer*), who constantly wars within himself because he is a vampire with a human soul. He seeks redemption of his past sins by playing detective and fending for the destitute with his helpers, Cordelia and other characters. In the fourth season of *Angel* (2002), Jasmine, portrayed by Charisma Carpenter and Gina Torres, is a powerful goddess who leaches off of human hosts, draining them of life force. She possesses different characters, including Cordelia, and masterminds much of the mischief in seasons one through four.

Angel Heart (1987) is a horror film written and directed Alan Parker and based on the novel *Falling Angel* by William Hjortsberg. It stars Mickey Rourke as Harry Angel, Robert De Niro as Louis Cyphre, and Lisa Bonet as Epiphany Proudfoot. Harry, a New York City private investigator, is hired by Louis Cyphre to find Johnny Favorite, a famous jazz singer whom Louis helped achieve fame. Johnny was last seen at a hospital, where he was being treated for shell shock for twelve years. Harry discovers he is not there and that a doctor was bribed to say he was. The doctor whom Harry is interrogating is found dead shortly after being questioned. Harry tracks more clues to New Orleans, where Johnny's lover, band member, and daughter are, but they turn up dead, too, after Harry questions them. Harry discovers that Johnny had made a deal with the devil—his soul in exchange for fame—but then performed a ritual to hide from the devil and keep the devil from collecting his due, which involved killing a soldier and eating his heart. His client shows up, and Harry figures out that Louis Cyphre is a homophone for Lucifer. It is revealed that Harry is Johnny and has actually been the one killing everyone in a fugue state.

Laurell K. Hamilton's Anita Blake: Vampire Hunter series (1993–) is set in a parallel universe where the supernatural is not cloaked, but openly part of everyone's reality, as exhibited by Anita Blake's profession. Anita is a professional vampire executioner, an animator (brings the dead back to life), and supernatural consultant for the police. She is also of German and Mexican descent and carries multiple strains of the lycanthropy virus, including wolf, leopard, lion, hyena, and tiger. The series of more than twenty-five books, which has also spawned into a comic book series as well as short stories, follows Anita as she solves supernatural crimes, navigates the personal and the political, and grows from viewing supernatural creatures as suspect to seeing supernatural creatures as possibly friends and even romantic partners.

Nisi Shawl's "At the Huts of Ajala" (2000) was published in *Dark Matter: A Century of Speculative Fiction from the African Diaspora.*

AVP: Alien vs. Predator (2004) is a science fiction action/adventure horror film written and directed by Paul W. S. Anderson with story by Dan O'Bannon, Ronald Shusett, Jim Thomas, and John Thomas. The film is a crossover of the *Alien* and *Predator* franchises, starring Sanaa Lathan as Alexa, the expert Arctic guide; Lance Henriksen as Charles, the billionaire archaeologist mission sponsor; and Raoul Bova as Sebastian, the hieroglyphic specialist. An archaeologist team discovers a submerged pyramid in the Arctic, where they happen upon an ancient sacrificial ritual involving Predators killing Aliens. By interpreting the hieroglyphics, the team ascertains that they have been bated in order to be body host to the new Aliens for the Predators to hunt. They must not only escape with their lives, but they must also attempt to keep the Aliens from escaping. Alexa and a Predator, Scar, are the only survivors, with Alexa sinking the Alien Queen into the ocean. A Predator ship returns to retrieve their comrade as well as reward Alexa with a Predator spear, acknowledging her warrior abilities. However, on board the Predator ship, Scar harbors an Alien chestburster.

The Believers (1987) is a horror film based on Nicholas Cone's novel *The Religion*, and is directed by John Schlesinger and written by Mark Frost. It stars Martin Sheen as Cal Jamison and Helen Shaver as Jessica Halliday. Cal is a recent widower and single father who moves to New York City to be a police psychologist. He treats Tom Lopez, who was undercover, trying to gather intelligence about a cult. Tom's babblings begin to make sense as ritualistic child sacrifices occur around the city by a group practicing a form of brujería. The group may also have more exclusive membership, including powerful New York elite. The case becomes even more personal for Cal when the cult targets his son.

In Toni Morrison's *Beloved* (1987), Sethe's home in Cincinnati is haunted by the revenant of her dead daughter, unnamed but known as Beloved, and the lingering violent consequences of slavery. Set after the Civil War, *Beloved* reveals how racism and the slave industry haunt all the characters, affecting Sethe's remaining children as well as the entire community. While Beloved forces most to flee the house—Sethe's other children and Paul D.—Sethe tries to appease Beloved out of guilt because Sethe believes that Beloved is the two-year-old daughter she killed. Sethe tried to escape her cruel white master but was nearly caught; she killed Beloved to keep her from being retaken by the plantation owner, believing death to be preferable to slavery. The attention causes Beloved to become more powerful and more ravenous. The women in the community help exorcise Beloved from Sethe's home, and Sethe comes to terms with her history.

Black Orpheus (1959) is a fantasy film based on the play *Orfeu da Conceição* by Vinicius de Moraes and is directed by Marcel Camus and written by Marcel Camus and Jacques Viot. It stars Breno Mellow as Orfeo and Marpessa Dawn as Eurydice. The film is a re-visioning of the Orpheus and Eurydice myth set in Rio de Janeiro. Eurydice is running from Death incarnate, and Orfeu is running from a lackluster engagement—and both end up running into each other's arms during Carnaval. Eurydice is tragically killed, and Orfeu descends into the basement under the Office of Missing Persons looking for her, where he witnesses a Macumba ritual. Eurydice speaks to him through an old woman, but as in the Greek myth, he gazes on her and her spirits leave forever. He retrieves her body from the morgue and carries her home, but he is killed by his jealous fiancée. Several children pick up his guitar and play it, believing that his guitar causes the sun to rise.

Blacula (1972) is a comedy horror Blaxploitation film directed by William Crain and written by Joan Torres and Raymond Koenig. It stars William Marshall as Blacula/Mamuwalde and Vonetta McGee as Luva. Mamuwalde is an African prince of the Abani nation who seeks Dracula's help in quelling the slave trade. Dracula refuses and turns Mamuwalde into a vampire, naming him Blacula and locking him in a coffin. That was in 1780. In 1972, interior decorators purchase the coffin and have it shipped to Los Angeles. Blacula arrives and is released, killing and turning people and being pursued by a police department pathologist. Blacula finds Luva, whom he believes is the reincarnated version of wife, and he turns her to save her life; however, Luva is killed. Desperate with grief, Blacula stands in the sunlight, committing vampire suicide.

Tite Kubo's Bleach (2001–) is a manga series that centers on Ichigo Kurosaki, a high schooler who was incidentally given Soul Reaper powers. The series chronicles his capers as a Soul Reaper, a soldier who escorts souls to the Soul Society after they depart from this world and battles Hollows, which are malevolent lost souls who threaten both humans and other souls. Yoruichi Shihōin is a former Shinigami captain in one of the Soul Society's highest-ranking noble families. She can transform into a cat at will, and she is renowned for her flash step ability, a high speed movement in combat.

Nnedi Okorafor's *The Book of Phoenix* (2015) is the prequel to *Who Fears Death* (2011). Phoenix is an "accelerated woman," a genetic experiment confined to Tower 7 in New York run by LifeGen, also known as Big Eye. She is only two years old but possesses the mind and body of a mature woman; however, she maintains a childlike innocence, that is, until her Saeed, a fellow "speciMen" and lover, kills himself because he witnesses something deeply disturbing in a forbidden part of the lab. Phoenix then must grow up, escaping and demolishing Tower 7. After her awakening, she journeys through time and space, witnessing the cruel machinery of Western colonialism at work and redressing those wrongs by destroying Big Eye facilities.

John Sayles's *The Brother from Another Planet* (1984) is a science fiction comedy film written and directed by John Sayles. It stars Joe Morton as The Brother and Daryl Edwards as Fly. The Brother, a mute black man from Another Planet, escapes his slave masters, seeking refuge in Harlem, Earth. Pursued by two white men in black who want to capture and return him to Another Planet, The Brother must evade them with his telekinetic powers. The comedy is stifled by intrusions of cruel realities, including The Brother's ability to sense the presence of past immigrants and their plights, as well as when The Brother stumbles upon the Harlem drug scene.

Paule Marshall's *Brown Girl, Brownstones* (1959) is set in Brooklyn in the 1930s and focuses on the coming-of-age narrative of Selina Boyce, an immigrant from Barbados whose family is trying to "make it" in America despite battling racism and poverty. Selina's mother, Silla, and father, Deighton, have oppositional personalities, with Silla being overly critical and Deighton being blithe and less fixated on getting a house (status symbol) than is his wife. Selina must navigate family drama, puberty, and racial tensions through the Great Depression and World War II, discovering her own sense of self and values.

In Nalo Hopkin's *Brown Girl in the Ring* (1998), economic collapse has the left the world in ruins and given rise to new localized orders. Inner city Toronto is run by Rudy Sheldon and his crew, performing favors for the city officials who have fled to the suburbs. The Premier Uttley of Ontario requires a heart transplant and charges Rudy with finding her a suitable donor. Meanwhile, on the city's outskirts, Ti-Jeanne cares for her newborn son and lives with her grandmother, Gros-Jeanne, an ancestral healer of the Obeah tradition. Tony, the father of Ti-Jeanne's child, shows up at Gros-Jeanne's home, asking for sanctuary, but in actuality he has been sent by Rudy to harvest Gros-Jeanne's heart. Rudy, who is revealed to be Gros-Jeanne's bitter ex-husband, summons a Duppy spirit to finish off Ti-Jeanne. Ti-Jeanne must use her grandmother's spiritual training to confront Rudy and make him pay for killing her grandmother. Premier Uttley has a change of heart, literally and figuratively, after receiving Gros-Jeanne's heart, vowing to make Toronto a better place for all, not just the elite.

Buffy the Vampire Slayer (1997–2003) is a television series created by Joss Whedon and stars Sara Michelle Gellar as Buffy; Anthony Stewart Head as Rupert Giles, the Watcher; David Boreanaz as Angel, Buffy's vampire lover; and Nicholas Brendon as Xander Harris, Alyson Hannigan as Willow Rosenberg, and Charisma Carpenter as Cordelia Chase, Buffy's friends and helpers collectively known as the "Scooby Gang." The seven seasons follow Buffy; her guide and trainer, Giles; and the "Scooby Gang" through high school and college as they repeatedly save the town of Sunnydale, and occasionally the world, from all manner of vampires, demons, and miscellaneous dark forces.

Chloe, Love Is Calling You (1934) is a pre-Code film directed and written by Marshall Neilan. It stars Olive Borden as Chloe and Reed Howes as Wade, Chloe's husband. Set in the South, the film features Chloe, a woman of supposedly mixed heritage, who lives with Mandy, her mammy. Chloe is ashamed of her mixed-race status and rejoices when she discovers that she is actually the long lost daughter of a white plantation owner, Colonel Gordon, who Mandy kidnapped because she believed the colonel was responsible for lynching her husband. Chloe is reunited with her father, but Mandy steals Chloe away again, this time to sacrifice her in a voodoo ritual. Wade, a white man, and Jim, a mixed-race man, save Chloe; but Jim dies saving Wade's life (and Chloe preferred Wade to Jim anyway because he was white).

Chesya Burke's "Chocolate Park" is a story in her collection of short stories, *Let's Play White* (2004).

Cleopatra Jones (1973) is a Blaxploitation action crime thriller film directed by Jack Starrett and written by Max Julien and Sheldon Keller. It stars Tamara Dobson as Cleopatra in the title role; Bernie Casey as Reuben, Cleopatra's lover and operator of a halfway house for addicts; and Shelley Winters as Mommy, a drug lord. Cleopatra drives a '73 Corvette Stingray fully equipped with weapons and has mad martial arts skills. She fronts as a model, but she is actually an undercover special agent for the U.S. government. After burning a Turkish poppy field belonging to Mommy, Cleopatra must return home to Los Angeles to save her boyfriend's halfway house and her own neighborhood from Mommy's fury.

Alice Walker's magnum opus *The Color Purple* (1982) is epistolary format with the protagonist, Celie, a poor adolescent in Georgia, writing to God because she is traumatized. Her step-father, Alphonso, physically and sexually abuses her, resulting in two pregnancies. He takes away her children and marries her off to malcontent widower, Mister, who needs someone to look after his children. Celie raises his children and helps her sister escape Alphonso, eventually also caring for Mister's mistress, Shug Avery, a jazz singer with whom Celie falls in love. Shug helps Celie recover her sister's letters, discovering that Nettie is living with a missionary couple who adopted Celie's two children. Celie musters up the courage to leave Mister and settle in Tennessee, working as a seamstress. Although Mister undergoes a change of heart, Celie refuses to reunite with him. When Alphonso dies, Celie inherits her home and moves back. Nettie, Celie's children, Shug, and a few other characters join her there.

W.E.B. Du Bois's "The Comet" (1920) is a science fiction short story originally published in *Darkwater: Voices from Within the Veil*. A comet hits Earth, releasing poisonous fumes and seemingly killing everyone except for a black man named Jim Davis and a white, wealthy woman named Julia. Jim and Julia are able to travel around New York City together without suspicion or threat, and they nearly have a tryst when Julia's father and a gang of white men show up interrupting them. Julia leaves Jim to join the white men, and the white men debate whether to lynch him or not, but concede since Jim saved Julia. A black woman, presumably his wife, runs into Jim's arms at the end of the story with her dead child in her arms.

Charles Waddell Chesnutt's *The Conjure Woman* (1899) is a collection of seven short pieces of fiction with the overarching frame of being narrated by Uncle Julius McAdoo to a white couple, John and Annie, who are thinking about buying and moving to an old plantation in the South. The stories are a variety of tales about unpleasant southern realities that the black characters face. Many are folk tales with Afrocentric supernatural elements, including Hoodoo. Uncle Julius's renditions of these stories contrast with John's romanticized ideas of the South.

Dean Koontz's novel *Darkfall* (1984), also known as *Darkness Comes*, follows Detective Jack Dawson as he mourns for the loss of his wife, cares for his two children, and attempts to solve a string of brutal murders. His partner, Rebecca, believes that the mutilated corpses are victims of mafia violence, but Jack believes the deaths are supernatural in nature due to the fact that the bodies are maimed as if by a vicious animal but are not eaten. He discovers that a bocor summoned the beings that are killing people. Jack also discovers their origin: a pit from hell in a shed, which grows as time passes, allowing larger demons to pass through. Jack may have to sacrifice himself in order to close the pit.

Dawn of the Dead (2004) is an action/adventure horror film directed by Zack Snyder and written by George A. Romero and James

Gunn. It stars Sarah Polley as Ana, a nurse, and Ving Rhames as Kenneth, a police sergeant. The film focuses on a group of random survivors who convene and fortify a mall during a zombie apocalypse. They must keep the zombies out, but they must also withstand the drama and turmoil within their confined group. As the group's numbers and supplies dwindle, they decide to make a run for it, escaping to where a member's boat is docked. Many perish along the way, and the few who make it to the boat and later the island on Lake Michigan are confronted with hordes of zombies. Their fate is left ambiguous.

Def by Temptation (1990) is a horror film written and directed by James Bond III. It also stars James Bond III as Joel, Kadeem Hardison as K, Cynthia Bond as the Seductress, and Bill Nunn as Dougy. Joel is having a crisis of faith and seeks advice from K, his friend in New York. They go barhopping, and Joel falls for an attractive woman, who is actually a succubus. Dougy and K must discover what the temptress is and how to kill her before their friend Joel succumbs to her deadly charms.

Octavia Butler's "The Evening and the Morning and the Night" is a novella originally published in *Omni* (1987). Cancer has been cured; however, the descendants of those who were cured develop Duryea-Gode Disease (DGD), a genetic ailment that induces violence and extreme mental disorders. Through strict diet, the bearers of the disease can delay symptoms, but due to the social alienation that the disease incurs and the impending doom, many ponder if life as a DGD carrier is worth living. Lynn is one of the youth who suffers from DGD and must endure its social stigma. She is marked by the food she eats as well as by an emblem she must wear. Lynn must balance her personal freedom with the good of the community and continually decide between autonomy or government mandates.

Zora Neale Huston's *Every Tongue Got to Confess: Negro Folk-tales from the Gulf States* (1929) is part anthropological project and part oral history manuscript. Hurston collected stories from African Americans in the Deep South in 1927, recording what she categorized as "God Tales," "Preacher Tales," "Devil Tales," "Witch and Hant Tales," "Heaven Tales," "John and Massa Tales," "Neatest Trick Tales," "Mistaken Identity Tales," "Fool Tales," "Woman Tales," "School Tales," "Miscellaneous Tales," "Talking Animal Tales," and "Animal Tales." These "confessions" stand as testament to the rich oral tradition of African Americans maintained in the South.

Evil Dead (2013) is the fourth horror film in the *Evil Dead* franchise directed by Fede Alvarez and written by Fede Alvarez, Rodo Sayagues, and Sam Raimi. It stars Jane Levy as Mia, Shiloh Fernandez as David, Lou Taylor Pucci as Eric, and Jessica Lucas as Olivia. A group of friends stay in remote cabin in the woods to support Mia as she attempts to fight heroin withdrawals. They find a book in the cellar, and Eric reads a passage, summoning an evil entity that possesses Mia. Mia tries to flee the cabin, but the others think her outburst is related to her drug addiction and stop her. Her possession worsens, and the group discovers from the book that she is under the influence of the Taker of Souls, who requires five souls in order to release the Abomination. After five members of the group are killed and Mia is left alone, she kills the Abomination with a chainsaw.

Extant (2014–2015) is a science fiction television drama created by Mickey Fisher and starring Halle Berry as Molly, Pierce Gagnon as Ethan, and Grace Gummer as Julie Gelineau. Molly is an astronaut who has spent thirteen months in space, only to return to Earth and discover she is pregnant, despite previously being infertile and on a solo mission. Her search for answers regarding "The Offspring" turns up disturbing and disorienting information, beginning with the fact that she was its host, not its mother.

"A Fool for Love" is episode seven in the *Buffy the Vampire Slayer* television series (1997–2003), season five. It originally aired on

November 4, 2000, and features guest actors David Boreanaz as Angelus, Julie Benz as Darla, Juliet Landau as Drusilla, and Kali Rocha as Cecily Addams. Angelus, Darla, and Drusilla are a dynasty of vampire who sired Spike. Cecily was Spike's human love interest in 1880 London who spurned him because of his lowly status. This episode recounts Spike's origin story as he explains to a morally and physically injured Buffy how Slayers have been killed in the past, or at least how he managed to kill two. Spike's two Slayer kills include a Chinese Slayer during the Boxer Rebellion in 1900 and Nikki Wood, a black woman Slayer, on a New York City subway in 1977. The information he provides upsets Buffy, who spurns him in much the same manner that Cecily did, which sends Spike into a vengeful rage. He recants and comforts Buffy when he finds her crying at her home because she has received bad news about her injuries and is coming to terms with her mortality.

Formation (2016) is a Beyoncé music video directed by Melina Matsoukas. Written by Khalif Brown, Jordan Frost, Asheton Hogan, Mike Will Made It, and Beyoncé, the song was released on February 16, 2016. The lyrics and images in the music video celebrate the formation of Beyoncé's black feminine identity as well as the formation of black femininity and black cultural identity as a whole, with references to southern heritage, Katrina, and the Black Lives Matter movement.

Freddy vs. Jason (2003) is a crossover horror film, combining the *Friday the 13th* and *A Nightmare on Elm Street* franchises, directed by Ronny Yu and written by Wes Craven, Victor Miller, Damian Shannon, and Mark Swift. It stars Robert Englund as Freddy, Ken Kirzinger as Jason, Monica Keena as Lori, Jason Ritter as Will, and Kelly Rowland as Kia. The teenagers of Springwood have forgotten about Freddy, causing him to lose his ability to terrorize them in their dreams. Freddy enlists Jason's aid, having him kill residents in their sleep and causing people to assume Freddy is back. However, Jason begins to off potential victims for Freddy;

thus, Freddy pulls Jason into his dream realm and battles him, having a decided advantage over the hockey-masked serial killer there. The teenagers realize what is going on and decide to help trick Freddy into their waking reality, hoping that Jason can finish him. Both killers appear to die, but at the end of the film, Jason emerges from the lake holding Freddy's winking decapitated head.

Foxy Brown (1974) is a Blaxploitation action crime thriller film written and directed by Jack Hill and starring Pam Grier in the title role as the vengeful and voluptuous woman tracking down her boyfriend's killers; Antonio Fargas as Link Brown, Foxy's treacherous brother; and Peter Brown as Steve Elias, the manager of a modeling agency linked to Foxy's boyfriend's death. Foxy goes undercover as a prostitute to discover who murdered her government agent boyfriend who was investigating drug dealers. She is caught and sent to a drug-manufacturing plant to be used as a sex-slave. After escaping, she organizes a grassroots squad to stop a drug deal and deliver Steve's genitals to his girlfriend, Kathryn, who had Foxy sent to a farm to be sexually assaulted.

"Ganger Ball Lightning" is from Nalo Hopkinson's collection of short fiction, *Skin Folk* (2001). A couple uses skin suits to experience what the other feels when they make love; however, they fail to adhere to the product's imperative directions.

Jewelle Gomez's *The Gilda Stories* (1990) begins in 1850s Louisiana but spans over 200 years in episodic time jumps. The protagonist, a lesbian and an escaped slave, finds refuge in a New Orleans brothel, where she is turned into a vampire by the Madame, the elder Gilda. After the elder Gilda opts for a true death, the protagonist becomes the current reigning Gilda. As an eternal being and as an intersectionally marginalized being (female, black, queer, vampire), her narrative explores personal and social issues within the context of extended time as well as reimagines the European vampire in an African framework.

Angela Toussaint returns to her family home in Tananarive Due's *The Good House* (2003) in Sacajawea, Washington, to put it on the market and rid herself of the unpleasant memories. The house has been in her family for four generations and is the place where her *grandmére* Marie performed her healing vodou rituals. But the Good House's reputation suffered after several unfortunate incidences, including Angela's mother committing suicide and Angela's son accidentally shooting himself with his father's gun. Angela also discovers that Marie's gifts were used in an act of vengeance, evoking an antagonistic spirit that has spread from the house to the surrounding community and her estranged husband, Tariq. Angela must contend with the house and all it embodies.

"Greedy Choke Puppy" is from Nalo Hopkinson's collection of short fiction, *Skin Folk* (2001). A grandmother recalls tales of soucouyants, but her granddaughter, who is now an educated woman, is not interested in such yarns anymore.

"A Habit of Waste" is from Nalo Hopkinson's collection of short fiction, *Skin Folk* (2001). Cynthia spies a woman with her original body on a streetcar. The woman flaunts her black body and curves confidently, but when Cynthia inhabited the body, she hid them in shame. Cynthia then begins to criticize her current white body model.

Halloween (1978) is a slasher horror film directed by John Carpenter and written by John Carpenter and Debra Hill, starring Donald Pleasence as Dr. Sam Loomis, Michael Myers's psychiatrist, and debuting Jamie Lee Curtis as Laurie Strode, Michael Myers's prime target. The film is the first installment of the *Halloween* franchise, explaining the origins of Michael Myers, who stalks and terrorizes characters with his iconic butcher knife and white mask. The film begins with six-year-old Michael stabbing his sister to death on Halloween night in 1963; it then jumps fifteen years later when he escapes on Halloween and returns to his hometown of Haddonfield, Illinois, where he embarks on a killing spree with Dr. Loomis in pursuit and Laurie just a few steps ahead. Laurie and Dr. Loomis both injure Michael, but his body is not found; hence, the nine sequels to date.

Hannibal (2013–2015) is a psychological thriller/crime drama horror television series spinoff of the Dr. Hannibal Lector book and film franchise created by Bryan Fuller and based on the characters by Thomas Harris. It stars Hugh Dancy as Will, Mads Mikkelsen as Hannibal, and Gina Torres as Bella Crawford. Will is an FBI profiler who has a gift for getting into the minds of psychopaths, but his gift takes a heavy toll on his mental and emotional well-being. Hannibal is a renowned psychiatrist solicited to mentor Will. The series explores their relationship, particularly Hannibal's attempts to turn Will into cannibalistic serial killer like himself.

Memphis Minnie's "Hoodoo Lady":

> Hoodoo lady, how do you do?
> They tell me you take a boot and turn it to a brand new shoe
> But don't put that thing on me
> Don't put that thing on me
> Don't put that thing on me
> 'Cause I'm going back to Tennessee
>
> Hoodoo lady, you can turn water to wine
> I been wondering where have you been all this time
> I'm setting here, broke, and I ain't got a dime
> You ought to put something in these dukes of mine
> But don't put that thing on me
> Don't put that thing on me
> Don't put that thing on me
> 'Cause I'm going back to Tennessee
>
> (spoken: Boy, you better watch it 'cause she's tricky.)

Hoodoo lady, I want you to unlock my door
So I can get in and get all my clothes
But don't put that thing on me
Don't put that thing on me
Don't put that thing on me
'Cause I'm going back to Tennessee

Now look-a here, Hoodoo lady, I want you to treat me right
Bring my man back home but don't let him stay all night
And don't put that thing on me
Don't put that thing on me
Don't put that thing on me
'Cause I'm going back to Tennessee

(spoken: Boy, she's tricky as she can be. Better watch her, too.)

Why look-a here, Hoodoo lady, I'm your friend
When you leave this time, come back again
But don't put that thing on me
Don't put that thing on me
Don't put that thing on me
'Cause I'm going back to Tennessee

(spoken: Boys, I'm scared of her.)

N. K. Jemisin's *The Hundred Thousand Kingdoms* (2010) is the first
entry of her fantasy Kingdom trilogy. *Kingdoms* revolves around
its protagonist, Yeine Darr, a tribal chieftain eventually thrust into
the dangerous politics of castle intrigue as she is invited to live in
the city of Sky ruled by her grandfather, the King. Yeine finds herself a pawn between the power struggles between her royal family
members and the pertinacious gods they have enslaved. Yeine must
navigate family politics, especially after Dekarta declares Yeine the
heir to his kingdom; however, she comes to realize that she is being
groomed as a sacrifice to the Skyfather by Dekarta to ensure his
rule and as a sacrifice to reincarnate as the goddess Enefa. Yeine

also must process the ideas that she was born to be this sacrifice, which will enable Enefa to restore balance to the universe and remove the chains of bondage from the gods, ensuring the kingdom's survival.

Stephen King's *It* (1987) is set in two different time periods, 1957–1958 and 1984–1985, in Derry, Maine. A group of misfit kids who call themselves the "Loser Club" encounter a malicious entity that can take the form of one's worst fears; however, it normally manifests as a clown named Pennywise that stalks the town's sewers. After suffering casualties, Loser Club defeats It, and vows to gather again and fight It if It returns. Twenty-seven years later, most of the group is abroad living their lives, when a string of heinous child-murders occurs in Derry. They reconvene to deal with their traumatic childhood memories, discovering that It arises every twenty-seven years to feed before going back into hibernation. They eventually destroy It, just as a storm destroys Derry, in essence, freeing the characters from the past.

I Walked with a Zombie (1943) is a horror film directed by Jacques Tourneur and written by Curt Siodmak, Ardel Wray, and Inez Wallace. It stars James Ellison as Wesley Rand, Paul's half-brother and employee; Frances Dee as Betsy Connell, a nurse hired to care for Paul's wife; and Tom Conway as Paul Holland, a Saint Sebastian sugar plantation owner. Complicated family dynamics plague the plantation: Wesley and Jessica, Paul's wife, are in love, and Betsy and Paul are attracted to each other. Jessica suffers from an unknown illness, and Betsy takes her to see the local voodoo practitioners, only to discover that the voodoo priest is Mrs. Rand, Wesley and Paul's mother. The locals suspect Jessica of being a zombie, and Mrs. Rand later admits to Betsy that she was possessed and put a curse on Jessica to keep Jessica from running away with Wesley and causing strife in the family. Under the influence of the Sabreur, Wesley stabs Jessica, then carries her into the sea where he drowns. Paul and Betsy are left to comfort each other.

The title character in Jonathan Mayberry's Joe Ledger series (2009–) is an Army Ranger veteran and detective based in Baltimore. Hired by the Department of Military Sciences (DMS), Joe's job is to pursue and eliminate advanced bio-terrorists' threats, which can take the form of deadly pathogens used to generate zombie flu or genocide or both. Joe encounters alien conspiracies, secret societies bent on ethnic cleansing or profit (such as the Seven Kings), as well as vampire assassins known as the Red Order as he and his fellow DMS members attempt to keep the world from descending into plague and chaos.

King of the Zombies (1941) is a comedy horror film directed by Jean Yarbrough and written by Lindsley Parsons. It stars Dick Purcell as Mac, Joan Woodbury as Barbara, and Mantan Moreland as the pilot's superstitious manservant, Jeff. A plane crashes on a Caribbean island, and a German doctor invites the passengers to stay in his mansion. Jeff tries to convince the other passengers that the doctor is harboring more than human guests in the doctor's abode. The passengers eventually discover the doctor is a spy overseeing a voodoo ritual and seeking intelligence on zombies that he can use as military weaponry.

Lemonade (2016) is Beyoncé's sixth studio album as well as the title of the one-hour HBO visual album directed by Beyoncé, Dikayl Rimmasch, and Jonas Åkerlund. Tidal, the streaming service co-owned by Beyoncé, describes the project as "every woman's journey of self-knowledge and healing." The film is divided into segments (Intuition, Denial, Anger, Apathy, Emptiness, Accountability, Reformation, Forgiveness, Resurrection, Hope, and Redemption), and it is interspersed with poetry by Warsan Shire. *Lemonade*'s lyrics and images address the personal as well as the political and the territory that spans between and connects the two.

Erna Brodber's *Louisiana* (1994) explores creole culture in both Louisianas—the state and the Jamaican parish—through the character of Ella Townsend, an African American anthropologist with Caribbean heritage researching Louisiana folk life. During her project, she discovers connections between previously partitioned places, like life and death, magic and religion, and the mystical and reality. Ella is particularly made aware of these correlations when her main research subject dies but continues to contact her after death through Ella's tape recorder. Ella learns about herself as well as the rich and fluid beliefs and practices of magico-religions.

Gloria Naylor's *Mama Day* (1988) is set in Willow Springs off the South Carolina and Georgia coasts. It is a community of emancipated slave descendants who have lived there for generations. Mama Day is the community's healer and a direct descendant of the community's founder, Saphira Wade. Mama Day's niece, Cocoa, is next in line and resembles Mama Day's headstrong personality. However, Cocoa is hexed by a jealous wife, and Mama Day must save her, but Cocoa's husband, a modern, Westernized man, must grapple with Mama Day's ancient ways and the community's decidedly unique culture in order to aid his wife.

Christopher Farnsworth's Nathaniel Cade series (2010–) features three novels and a novella: *Blood Oath* (2010), *The President's Vampire* (2011), *Red, White, and Blood* (2012), and *The Burning Men* (2014). The series centers on Nathaniel Cade, a vampire who has been bound by a voodoo blood oath to serve and protect the president of the United States since Andrew Jackson. Cade and Zach Barrows, Cade's official White House handler, tackle cases that are "above top secret," saving the country and the world from the real monsters that inspired the myths.

Night of the Living Dead (1968) is an independent horror film directed by George A. Romero and written by John A. Russo and George A. Romero. It stars Duane Jones as Ben and Judith O'Dea as Barbra. The film is set in rural Pennsylvania, where Barbra and her brother, Johnny, go to visit their father's grave. They are attacked by a strange, menacing man, and Johnny is killed. Barbra flees to a farmhouse, where Ben appears and fends off the onslaught of shuffling corpses, saving Barbra and locking them in the farmhouse with others seeking refuge. After an attempt to escape fails and the animated corpses break into the house, Ben, the only remaining survivor, locks himself in the cellar. The next morning, a makeshift militia kills Ben, assuming he is one of the activated dead.

Nosferatu (1922) is a horror film based on Bram Stoker's *Dracula* directed by F. W. Murnau and written by Henrik Galeen. It stars Max Schreck as Count Orlok, Gustav von Wangenheim as Thomas Hutter, and Greta Schroder as Ellen. The storyline parallels *Dracula*, with Thomas traveling to Transylvania to broker a real-estate deal with Count Orlok, and Count Orlok becoming enamored with Thomas's fiancée, Ellen. The Count arrives in England, after killing everyone on board the ship, and strange deaths begin occurring in the town he ports. The end slightly departs from *Dracula*'s template, with Ellen sacrificing herself to kill the nosferatu.

Ouanga (1936) is a horror film written and directed by George Terwilliger and stars Fredi Washington as Clelie, the black Haitian plantation owner; Philip Brandon as Adam, the white neighboring plantation owner; and Marie Paxton as Eve, Adam's fiancé. Adams spurns Clelie because she "belongs with her kind." Thus, Clelie attempts to put a curse, a ouanga (pronounced "wanga"), on Eve. When that does not work as expected, Clelie raises two zombies and has them kidnap Eve, whom she plans on sacrificing in a voodoo ritual. Lestrange, a black man, saves Eve and kills Clelie.

Prom Night (1980) is a slasher horror film based on a story by Robert Guza Jr., directed by Paul Lynch, and written by William Gray. It stars Leslie Nielsen as Mr. Hammond, the high school principal and Robin's father, and Jamie Lee Curtis as Kim Hammond, Robin's sister. It is 1980, the night of the prom, and the sixth anniversary of Robin Hammond's mysterious death, which was blamed on a local sexual predator. Four teenagers—Wendy, Jude, Kelly, and Nick—receive strange phone calls as they prepare for prom, and that night at the dance, a masked stranger picks the four teenagers off one by one. To save Nick (her date), Kim strikes the fatal blow, only to realize that the masked killer is her brother, Alex, who was also Robin's twin. Alex explains that the four teenagers were responsible for Robin's death before dying in Kim's arms.

Kiini Ibura Salaam's short story "Rosamojo" is from the anthology *Mojo: Conjure Stories* (2003), edited by Nalo Hopkinson.

Return of the Living Dead is a five comedy horror film series spawned from *Night of the Living Dead* (1968), but distinct from George A. Romero's sequels. The first film in the series is *The Return of the Living Dead* (1985) directed by Dan O'Bannon and written by Rudy Ricci, John A. Russo, Russell Streiner, and Dan O'Bannon. A Trioxin gas leak at a medical supply warehouse causes the dead to rise and attack humans to eat their brains. *Return of the Living Dead Part II* (1988) is written and directed by Ken Wiederhorn. A barrel of Trioxin gas leftover from the first film is discovered by a few kids, who accidentally unleash it, wreaking havoc on their town. *Return of the Living Dead Part III* (1993) is directed by Brian Yuzna and written by John Penney. A teenager witnesses his father, a colonel in the army use, Trioxin. When the young man's girlfriend is killed in a motorcycle accident, he uses the gas to bring her back to life. *Return of the Living Dead: Necropolis* (2005) is directed by Ellory Elkayem and written by William Butler and Aaron Strongoni. Set ten years after the previous film, a group of teens jailbreak their friend who is imprisoned at the lab where scientists are experimenting with Trioxin on zombie clones. During the effort to rescue their friends, the teens also release the zombies. *Return of the Living Dead: Rave to the Grave* (2005) is also directed by Ellory Elkayem and written by William Butler and Aaron Strongoni. Set one year after the previous film, the characters who were teenagers in *Necropolis* are now college students. Trioxin is now in capsule form as a recreational drug called Z; however, users eventually turn into zombies with prolonged use or high dosage.

Rigamo (2016) is a short film written and directed by Che Grayson and is based off the comic by Che Grayson and Sharon de la Cruz. It stars Judianny Compres as Isabelle, Akira Golz as Kera (age nine), and Chiquita Camille as Caroline. Kera Moore is a young, female superhero. She can bring the dead back to life with her tears, but she discovers that this superpower comes at a high price, costing her years of her own life: every time she brings something back from the dead, she advances in her own age.

Stephen King's *Salem's Lot* (1975) is short for Jerusalem's Lot, Maine, were the novel is set. Ben Mears returns home to Salem's Lot with the intent to write a novel about the town, particularly about a haunted house there where he saw a ghost as a child. Other mysterious characters take up residence—namely, Richard Straker and Barlow, who purchase the haunted house and Laundromat, converting it into an antique shop. People begin to go missing, and Ben and a small group of other townspeople deduce that the denizens of Salem's Lot are being turned into vampires. Ben and his band of renegades kill Barlow, the master vampire, but suffer casualties until only Ben and Mark remain. Ben and Mark flee to Mexico but return a year later during the day to set fire to the town.

Nalo Hopkinson's *The Salt Roads* (2003) interweaves three different narratives: that of Mer, a Haitian sugar plantation slave; Jeanne Duval, mistress of poet Charles Baudelaire in France; and Meritet, a Nubian prostitute turned St. Mary of Egypt. All three narratives and characters are guided and united by Lasirén, a fertility goddess who moves through time and space, offering her assistance to these three women as they seek freedom and autonomy. Lasirén aids Mer during the Haitian Revolution, helping her obtain a different type of freedom—one of preserved legacy. Lasirén then assists Jeanne in finding economic liberty and contentment, and finally, she helps Meritet transcend her circumstances and surroundings, freeing her mind, as she wanders the desert in communion with the goddess.

Scream Blacula Scream (1973) is the sequel to *Blacula* and is directed by Bob Kelljan and written by Joan Torres, Raymond Koenig, and Maurice Jules. William Marshall reprises his role as Blacula and is joined by Pam Grier as Lisa, a voodoo queen apprentice. Blacula is brought back into being by Willis, the disinherited son of a Voodoo queen. Blacula turns Willis as well as others into vampires and seeks Lisa's help, wishing to be cured of vampirism. As she performs the ritual, police search for the person responsible for recent murders. Blacula brutally kills one of the officers, and Lisa stabs the voodoo dolls made in his image, abolishing Blacula forever.

Scream 2 (1997) is a slasher horror film directed by Wes Craven, written by Kevin Williamson, and stars David Arquette, Neve Campbell, Courteney Cox, and Sarah Michelle Gellar. The film is set two years after the events of the first *Scream* and involves a copycat Ghostface serial killer taking out a group of college students who have the same names as the original victims. Several of the survivors from the Woodsboro murders help the police try to discover that the killers are, once again, a pair of psychopaths, one vying for fame, the other for revenge.

The Serpent and the Rainbow (1988) is directed by Wes Craven and written by Wade Davis, Richard Maxwell, and Adam Rodman. It is based on Wade Davis's nonfiction account of his investigation into a zombie claim in Haiti and stars Bill Pullman as Dennis Alan, Cathy Tyson as Marielle Duchamp, and Zakes Mokae as Dargent Peytraud. Dennis is commissioned by a pharmaceutical company to find the drug used in Voodoo rituals to create zombies, believing that it has potential as an anesthetic. He searches in Haiti during a revolution, and is captured several times and tortured by the commander of the Tonton Macoute, Captain Dargent Petraud. A local witch doctor named Mozart sneaks Alan the drug, but back in the states, Alan is visited by Petraud's spirit, predicting his death. Thus, Alan returns to Haiti, where his allies are sacrificed for Petraud's political and personal power. Alan is dusted with zombie power and buried alive. Alan eventually escapes his coffin and defeats Petraud with the help of Alan's jaguar spirit animal at the same time that Jean-Claude Duvalier is removed from power.

Stephen King's *The Shining* (1977) records Jack Torrance's descent into madness under the supernatural influences of a historic hotel in the Colorado Rockies. Jack is an author, an alcoholic, a husband, a father, an off-season hotel caretaker, as well as a person with anger management issues. His son, Danny, has "the shining," a unique psychic ability to see the hotel's less-than-scenic past, read minds, and receive premonitions. Danny's presence in the hotel extenuates the hauntings, and these malevolent forces eventually possess Jack. Induced by the hotel's hostel side, Jack attempts to kill his wife, Wendy, and Danny. They barely escape as Jack is killed in a boiler explosion, which also destroys the hotel.

Nalo Hopkinson's novel *Sister Mine* (2013) tells the story of two sisters fathered by a god and a mortal woman who were turned into a mortal human and a lake monster for their copulation. The sisters are conjoined in the womb, and separated only after birth. Abby is magical, but Makeda lacks mojo, which makes her an outsider in her own family during her childhood. When she is grown, Makeda decides to move out, away from her sister, in order to find her purpose and gifts since she is not magically endowed. Her father goes missing, so she returns home, only in time for him to die shortly after being found. It is revealed that Makeda did have mojo, but her uncle discarded it when he separated her from her sister at birth in order to house her father's mojo within her. After departing from her father's body, her father's disoriented spirit indwells a kudzu plant, searching for its lost mojo. Makeda, with her sister's help, embarks on a new quest: she must find her mojo in order to survive the reclaiming of her father's powers by his unsettled spirit.

Nalo Hopkinson's *Skin Folk* (2001) is a short fiction collection of fifteen narratives and winner of the 2002 World Fantasy Award for

Best Story Collection. The collection draws from Caribbean folk-lore, including the soucouyant (vampire) and the lagahoo (were-wolf). From reworkings of Red Riding Hood to postapocalyptic settings to science fiction melded with Caribbean points of view, *Skin Folk* explores in compressed form various aspects of what it means to inhabit one's skin.

Sleepy Hollow (2013–) is a television show based on Washing Irving's short story "The Legend of Sleepy Hollow" and is created by Alex Kurtzman, Roberto Orci, Phillip Iscove, and Len Wiseman. It stars Tom Mison as Ichabod Crane, a soldier spy during the American Revolution who kills the Headless Horseman in 1781, and Nicole Beharie as Abbi Mills, a police lieutenant in present day. Two hundred and thirty years after Ichabod and the Headless Horseman kill each other, the Headless Horseman is summoned back to life, bringing Ichabod with him because their bloods mixed when they died. The Headless Horseman is one of the Four Horsemen of the Apocalypse; thus, Ichabod solicits the aid of Abbie to help him stop the Headless Horseman's unholy mission.

Atsushi Ōkubo's Soul Eaters (2004–2013) is a Japanese manga series set in the Death Weapon Meister Academy in Death City, Nevada, where a Shinigami named Death trains humans who can shapeshift into weapons. These humans are called meisters, and they must acquire ninety-nine evil human souls and one witch in order to evolve their weapon into a death scythe, a Shinigami level weaponry. Mira Naigus is a meister. Her name is similar to the Japanese word for mummy, and she always appears wrapped in bandages.

Derrick Bell's "The Space Traders" (1992) is a science fiction short story that posits a provocative political debate. Extraterrestrials have made contact, brokering a trade agreement: they will give the United States unprecedented technical knowledge, including clean nuclear power, in exchange for all the black people. U.S. leaders debate the merits of the barter deal, eventually finding a way to perform rhetorical and policy gymnastics in order to legally make the exchange. The short story was adapted for an HBO television film in 1994.

The Spook Who Sat by the Door (1973) is a political satire film based on the novel by Sam Greenlee, directed by Ivan Dixon, and adapted to the screen by Sam Greenlee and Melvin Clay. It stars Lawrence Cook as Dan Freeman. Dan is the token black hire by the CIA in the 1970s. Unbeknownst to the CIA, Dan is also a black nationalist. After he is thoroughly trained in CIA tactics, he resigns, returns to Chicago, and begins training "Freedom Fighters" with the intent of making a "new nation" where black people have fairer opportunities and justice.

Sugar Hill (1974) is an action/adventure horror film directed by Paul Maslansky and written by Tim Kelly. It stars Marki Bey as Diana "Sugar," Zara Cully as Mama Maitresse, Robert Quarry as Morgan, and Don Pedro Colley as Lord of the Dead Baron Samedi. Sugar's boyfriend is murdered by white gangsters, who are also trying to take over her club. Mama Maitresse uses voodoo powers to summon Baron Samedi, who, in turn, raises zombies to stop the white gangsters' tirade in exchange for Sugar's soul.

Toni Morrison's *Sula* (1973) is set in The Bottom, a black neighborhood in Ohio, where Sula and Nel grow up together, the best of friends sharing a dark secret. Sula's family is less conventional, while Nel's family is mostly traditional and stable. Nel follows her mother's footsteps and settles down after high school, but Sula takes a ten-year sabbatical from mundane life. She returns in infamy and has an affair with Nel's husband. The town considers her the ultimate form of lewdness, ironically achieving a form of harmony with Sula's extreme disregard for convention there to balance them out. After Sula dies, the town loses its unity and disintegrates back to its usually petty bickering.

Supernova (2000) is a science fiction horror film directed by Walter Hill (credited as Thomas Lee) and written by David C. Wilson,

William Malone, and Daniel Chuba. It stars James Spader as copilot Nick, Angela Bassett as medical officer Kaela, Robert Forster as Captain A.J., Lou Diamond Phillips as medical technician Yerzy, Robin Tunney as paramedic Danika, Wilson Cruz as computer technician Benjamin, and Peter Facinelli as Kaela's former abusive love interest, Karl. The film is set in the twenty-second century and centers on the *Nightingale 229* medical crew. The search and rescue team answers a distress signal from Titan 37 moon, but encounters ship damage upon arrival. They still manage to save Karl, who initially signaled them, and an alien artifact in his possession that imbues him with strength and youth. Karl kills everyone except Nick and Kaela, but the surviving couple eventually destroy Karl and the alien artifact and escape back to Earth; however, the destruction of the alien artifact and the manner of their escape have lingering consequences for them and for the future of Earth.

Tales from the Crypt: Demon Night (1995) is a horror film spawned from the HBO series *Tales from the Crypt* and is directed by Ernest R. Dickerson and written by Ethan Reiff, Cyrus Voris, and Mark Bishop. It stars John Kassir as the Crypt Keeper (voice), Billy Zane as the Collector, William Sadler as Frank, and Jada Pinkett Smith as Jeryline. The Collector pursues Frank, who possesses an ancient and powerful artifact. Their cars crash, and they end up at a boardinghouse in rural New Mexico. Police get involved because both vehicles were stolen, but when the officers try and arrest the Collector and Frank, the Collector kills one of the officers, then creates a small demonic army from the sand and his own blood. Frank uses his artifact to protect the boardinghouse and convinces the residents that they must wait out the night. The night is spent battling the Collector's demonic army and ends with the Collector killing most of the people and Jeryline killing the Collector. Frank bestows the artifact to Jeryline before dying, and Jeryline leaves on a bus with it, pursued by the next Collector.

William Shakespeare's play *The Tempest* is about the scheming sorcerer Prospero's attempt to regain his deposed position as Duke of

Milan. After being exiled with his daughter, Miranda, to a remote island, Prospero enslaves Caliban and Ariel to do his bidding. Ariel is an island sprite who was previously enslaved by Sycorax, the unseen, powerful Algerian witch and mother of Caliban. A tempest conjured by Prospero causes a ship to wreck, washing several important persons ashore: Antonio, Prospero's usurping brother; King Alonso of Naples, who can restore Prospero to his proper place; and King Alonso's son, Ferdinand. Through Prospero's magical wiles and the fumbling aid of his minions, Caliban and Ariel, he reveals Antonio's treachery, regains his title, and further cements his station by orchestrating the marriage between Miranda and Ferdinand.

True Blood (2008–2014) is an HBO television series created by Alan Ball and based on Charlaine Harris's The Southern Vampire Mysteries book series. It stars Anna Paquin as Sookie, a telepathic waitress who is also part fairy; Stephen Moyer as Bill, a vampire from the Civil War era; Sam Trammel as Sam, a shapeshifting bar owner; Ryan Kwanten as Jason, Sookie's brother; and Rutina Wesley as Tara, Sookie's spunky best friend and later vampire. It is set mostly in a small town in Louisiana, beginning shortly after the creation of True Blood, a synthetic substitute for blood. True Blood allows vampires to emerge from hiding and forces society to adjust to the revelation that they exist. Each season reveals more supernatural beings living among humans as well as explores contemporary issues, such as religion and the power of belief, the violent consequences of racism and discrimination, human/non-human rights, as well as others.

Henry James' novel *The Turn of the Screw* (1898) is designed to conjure doubts and disorientation through its unreliable narrator. In the form of a found manuscript, the narrative is told from the perspective of a governess who has been hired by a wealthy man to manage his wards—his niece, Flora, and nephew, Miles. He leaves them all at his country estate in Bly, making it clear to the governess that he does not wish to be bothered with them.

Miles is expelled from boarding school for unknown reasons, but the governess is taken with him, so she does not pressure him into revealing the cause. She begins seeing a man and woman on the premise that the rest of the staff does not and believes the children see them as well. She surmises that they are the former governess, Miss Jessel, and another employee, Peter Quint, who had an affair and died there. The children seem to have an increasing affinity with the ghosts, and the governess must do everything in her power to protect them. In a final encounter with Peter Quint's ghost, Miles dies in the governess's arms.

Stephen King's *Under the Dome: A Novel* (2009) portrays from multiple points of view how the residents of Chester Mill, Maine, react to an encompassing, invisible dome being placed over their town, isolating them from the outside and acting as a crucible for small town politics and big egos. The chief of police is killed when the dome sets, leaving a key position of authority open for the ambitious Big Jim, a used car salesmen, to take over. A small group tries to repel Big Jim and his posse, but is forced to seek refuge on an abandoned farm. During Big Jim and Chef Bushey's drug battle, most of the townspeople are incinerated in an explosion. The few remaining are asphyxiating, when Barbie and Julia, two members of the resistance, go to an alien device they found that can communicate with the extraterrestrial owners and operators of the dome. After desperate pleas, they convince the aliens that they are sentient beings. The aliens remove the dome, which turns out to be something similar to an ant farm: solely for entertainment value.

Vamp (1986) is a comedy horror film directed by Richard Wenk and written by Richard Wenk and Donald P. Borchers. The film stars Chris Makepeace as Keith, Sandy Baron as Vic, Robert Rusler as A.J., Dedee Pfeiffer as Allison/Amaretto, Gedde Watanabe as Duncan, and Grace Jones as Queen Katrina. Three college students—Keith, A.J. and Duncan—embark on a comedy of errors in order to get into a fraternity by hiring a stripper to impress their college peers. Queen Katrina, the exotic dancer they attempt to hire, is entrancing and, as they discover, also a vampire. Escapades ensue as A.J. is killed and turned and Keith and Duncan befriend a waitress, Amaretto, who helps them flee the onslaught of vampires lead by Queen Katrina and Vlad.

The Vampire Diaries (2009–) is a teen romance television series developed by Kevin Williamson and Julie Plec and based on L. J. Smith's The Vampire Diaries book series. It stars Paul Wesley as Stefan, Ian Somerhalder as Damon, Nina Dobrev as Elena, and Kat Graham as Bonnie. The teen romance series centers on the love triangle between Elene, Stefan, and Damon—a human young woman and two brother vampires. In addition to their romantic drama, the setting, Mystic Falls, Virginia, has a long supernatural history that still affects the residents, who are mostly descendants of the original settlers. Bonnie, Elena's best friend and a powerful witch, dies in season four but returns as a ghost and is later resurrected.

L. A. Banks's twelve-book The Vampire Huntress Legend series (2003–2009) follows the escapades of Damali Richards, a spoken-word artist for Warriors of Light Records and a Neteru, a human born once a millennia to battle creatures from the Dark Realm, mainly vampires. Damali and her Guardian team throughout the series carry on the struggle between good and evil.

Wake (2010) is a short dramatic horror film written and directed by Bree Newsome and starring Sahr Ali as Charmaine, Christina Faison as Florence, and Benton Greene as The Man. Set in the South during the 1930s, the film depicts a sexually repressed woman, Charmain, who kills her father in order to be free of his patriarchal domination. She keeps dirt from her father's grave and uses it to conjure a spirit, requesting that the spirit give her the man of her dreams. The Man arrives on her porch and, at first, seems to meet all her criteria. However, the honeymoon phase does not last long. Charmaine finds herself, once again, under the rule of a cruel manlike entity with which she must contend.

The Walking Dead (2003–) is a comic book series written by Robert Kirkman and artistically rendered by Tony Moore and Charlie Adiard that has spawned a television series and video games. The series' nucleolus narrative follows Deputy Rick Grimes, who awoke from a coma after the zombie apocalypse occurred. He finds his wife, son, and other survivors, and together as a community they must endure the new reality of living among the walking dead.

The Walking Dead (2010–) television series is developed by Frank Darabont and is based on the comic book series by Robert Kirkman, Tony Moore, and Charlie Adlard. It stars Andrew Lincoln as Rick Grimes, former deputy; Steven Yeun as Glenn, a former pizza delivery guy and Maggie's husband; Norman Reedus as Daryl, a crossbow-wielding, motorcycle-riding hunter; Melissa McBride as Carol, an ex-domesticate who is now one of the fiercest characters; Lennie James as Morgan, a bō fighter who still believes in the potential for good in humanity; Lauren Cohan as Maggie, Glenn's girlfriend and the group's rising diplomatic leader; and Danai Gurira as Michonne, a pensive and capable katana warrior. The series follows the group under the (sometimes tentative) leadership of Rick as they try to survive the zombie apocalypse and establish a stable community amid the walking dead and equally dangerous living.

White Zombie (1932) is a pre-Code horror film directed by Victor Halperin and written by Garnett Weston. It is based on William Seabrook's *The Magic Island* and is often considered the first feature length zombie film. It stars Bela Lugosi as Murder Legendre, a voodoo master; Madge Bellamy as Madeline Short Parker, the damsel of interest; and Joseph Cathorn as Dr. Bruner, a missionary. A wealthy sugar plantation owner, Charles Beaumont, hires Murder Legendre to turn Madeline into a zombie in order to make her new husband believe she is dead so Charles can have her all to himself. Madeline appears to die, but when Neil, her mourning husband, visits her tomb and finds it empty, he ask Dr. Bruner to help him discover what happened to her. Dr. Bruner explains that Murder creates zombies that work and guard Charles's plantation. They go in search of Madeline, and while trying to rescue her, cause the death of Murder and Charles. Once Murder is dead, his control over Madeline is relinquished.

Octavia Butler's *Wild Seed* (1980) is the fourth book of the Patternist series but the earlier in terms of chronology. Anyanwu, a shapeshifting immortal from Africa with the ability to heal the sick and herself, is befriended by Doro, a bodysnatching immortal from Egypt. Doro has a colony where he practices eugenics, breeding gifted "seeds" together in order to create superior humans with whose bodies he can mate as well as snatch. He convinces Anyanwu to join him in his New World village, where he will bestow her with immortal children. Once there, he pairs her with his son Isaac. Power struggles ensue between Anyanwu and Doro after the death of Isaac and Nweke, Anyanwu and Isaac's daughter. She shifts into an animal and flees (because Doro cannot sense her or kill her when she is in animal form), and she establishes her own colony in Louisiana. Doro eventually finds her and disrupts her harmonious community, but he recants once she threatens to commit suicide. His concession of cruelty and power allows them to form a partnership.

Notes

Preface

1. I continue to employ this method in my initial viewings of horror movies. I remain terrified at the first viewing; it is the second viewing that gives me power, a sense of control over my emotions along with an ability to see the construction and seams of the film itself. The advent of the director's commentary on DVDs has only aided this process.

2. Yes, I was a womanish enough seven-year-old to use the word "heck" correctly.

3. I believe my older cousin Lee had a strange fixation on terrifying me— as older boy cousins/play brothers are wont to do with their annoying younger girl cousins/play sisters—and introduced me to the campier and far scarier Return of the Living Dead (1985–) series before my aunts rectified the situation by initiating my love for zombies by introducing me to George Romero, writer and director of *Night of the Living Dead* (1968).

4. Sanaa Lathan's character in *AVP*, Alexa Woods, is the only human survivor and teams up with the surviving Predator to defeat the Alien Queen and her minions.

5. The infected—the contagious peoples of the apocalypse in *28 Days Later*—are often mistakenly referred to as zombies. I am not so much of a zombie purist that I can't identify Boyle's contemporary reimagining of the human fear of contagion. His revised zombies are living beings infected with the dangerous virus named Rage.

6. The circumstance of Michonne's rape remains a controversial story arc in Robert Kirkman's comic book series. Michonne and two other (male)

members of her group are captured by a rival faction of survivors and tortured for information on their group's location and supply status.

7. The Vampire Huntress Legend series (2003–2009).

Introduction

1. The other genre is comedy.
2. Isabel Cristina Piñedo, *Recreational Terror: Women and the Pleasures of Horror Film Viewing* (New York: State University of New York Press, 1997), 31.
3. Cheryl Wall presents the concept of "worrying the lines" as a framework for reading African diasporic women's literature in that it is "inevitably a trope for repetition with difference. . . . [It] locates black women's writing in relation to the multiple literary traditions that inform it. . . . By rewriting or reading the dominant story, and delegitimating or displacing that story, black women inscribe their own." Cheryl W. Wall, Worrying *the Line: Black Women Writers, Lineage, and Literary Tradition* (Chapel Hill: University of North Carolina Press, 2005), 16.
4. Piñedo, *Recreational Terror*, 17.
5. Ibid., 18.
6. Ibid.
7. Ibid., 17.
8. Ibid.
9. Ibid.
10. Art-horror is directly opposed to what Carroll defines as natural horror, which he believes consists of the horrific actions society commits against itself, such as slavery, genocide, and war.
11. Much of contemporary theory makes this very same mistake. Most bookstores and other cultural markers refer to the subgenres together with the shaky use of grammatical slashes to highlight their differences, such as science fiction/fantasy/horror. I myself have been guilty of this particular notion, teaching courses with titles such as "Black Women in Science Fiction/Fantasy/Horror." Wall, *Worrying the Line*.
12. Noël Carroll, *The Philosophy of Horror: Or, Paradoxes of the Heart* (New York: Routledge, 1990), 27.
13. Ibid., 28–29.

14. Robin Wood, "The American Nightmare: Horror in the 70s," in *Horror, The Film Reader*, ed. Mark Jancovich (New York: Routledge, 2001), 26.

15. *Dawn of the Dead* (2004) is not one of the primary texts in this piece. It is used as an exemplar of the major barriers to black women in zombie horror—in particular, the presence and complicated characterizations of black female characters. Eight years later, Snyder's remake remains the highest-grossing zombie film of all time (boxofficemojo.com).

16. See Michael Newbury, "Fast Zombie/Slow Zombie: Food Writing, Horror Movies, and Agribusiness Apocalypse," *American Literary History* 24, no. 1: 87–114, 89.

17. *Dawn of the Dead* is not the only guilty party here. It proves useful because it is well known and the most contemporary example of my critical examinations at the time of writing.

18. The trope of the competent black male survivor who often aims to become a leader of the group emerged in George Romero's *Night of the Living Dead* (1968) with Duane Jones's Ben. See Adam Lowenstein's "Living Dead: Fearful Attractions of Film" (2010), Annalee Newitz's *Pretend We're Dead* (2006), and Kim Paffenroth's *Gospel of the Living Dead: George Romero's Visions of Hell on Earth* (2006) for critical analyses of Ben.

19. Snyder's construction of capable female survivors continues the revision Romero has sustained with the "representations of active and even aggressive women" in the rest of his "Dead" series. Stephen Harper, "'They're Us': Representations of Women in George Romero's 'Living Dead' Series," *Intensities: The Journal of Cult Media* 3 (2003): 1–12.

20. I begin in this century because Shakespeare's dramas remain an influential and foundational example of the modern Anglophone literary arts.

21. Sylvia Wynter, "Beyond Miranda's Meanings: Un/Silencing The 'Demonic Ground' of Caliban's 'Woman,'" in *Out of the Kumbla: Caribbean Women and Literature*, ed. Carole Boyce Davies and Elaine Savory Fido (Trenton, NJ: African World Press, 1994), 114–115.

22. Sycorax is Caliban's mother in Shakespeare's *The Tempest* and former ruler of the island Prospero has colonized. She is never seen or heard and is remembered by the island's inhabitants as monstrous in nature.

23. bell hooks, "The Oppositional Gaze: Black Female Spectators," *The Feminism and Visual Cultural Reader* (2003): 94–105.

24. William Shakespeare, *The Tempest*, Act I, Scene II.

25. Wood, "American Nightmare," 26.

26. Carol Clover speaks of this phenomenon as the "majority viewer" of horror film who is a young male. I extend his identity further to include that he is also white, heterosexual, and middle-class. See the first chapter of Carol J. Clover, *Men, Women, and Chain Saws: Gender in the Modern Horror Film* (Princeton, NJ: Princeton University Press, 1992). Harry Benshoff refers to this ideal viewer—though not exactly by that term— as he expands the definition of queerness to include those audience members who do not fit that very narrow ideal; see Harry Benshoff, "Blaxploitation Horror Films: Generic Reappropriation or Reinscription?" *Cinema Journal* 39, no. 2 (2000): 32–33.

27. Gloria T. Hull, Patricia Bell Scott, and Barbara Smith, eds., *But Some of Us Are Brave: All the Women Are White, All the Blacks Are Men: Black Women's Studies* (New York: Feminist Press at CUNY, 1993), i. I define text to include films, books, comics, and graphic novels as well as other mediums, such as painting, sculpture, and movie posters that can be interrogated by horror criticism. For this work, I focus on both film and comic book texts.

28. The excoriation of Michelle Obama's presentation as a First Lady as a wife and mother first, as well as a paragon of the institutional family, failed to acknowledge that her presentations subvert previous presentations of black women only as domestic workers. See Brittney Cooper, "Lay off Michelle Obama: Why White Feminists Need to Lean Back," *Salon*, November 29, 2013. Black womanhood has always been constructed as "strong" enough to handle men's work. Enslaved black women completed the same tasks as enslaved black men, for their work was not gendered. This aided the successful campaign to masculinize black women. See Hortense J. Spillers, "Mama's Baby, Papa's Maybe: An American Grammar Book," *diacritics* 17, no. 2 (1987): 65–81.

29. Carol Boyce-Davies, *Black Women, Writing and Identity: Migrations of the Subject* (New York: Routledge, 1994), 6.

30. bell hooks, "The Oppositional Gaze," in *Black Looks: Race and Representation* (New York: Routledge, 1992), 116.

31. Robin R. Means Coleman, *Horror Noire: Blacks in American Horror Films from the 1890s to Present* (New York: Routledge, 2013), location 766 of 8596.

32. http://www.graveyardshiftsisters.com/2016/01/presentations-black-women-in-horror.html.

33. Ibid.

34. Location 3460 of 8596.

35. Ibid.

36. This book contains an appendix with a short summary of each of the creative works analyzed through the text.

37. Matt Wray defines stigmatype in the following way: "Stigmatype is perhaps an odd neologism, but I coined it because stereotype, a tired word that connotes psychological prejudices and thought patterns, doesn't speak well to the social dimensions of cultural differentiation and because stigmatizing boundary term is too cumbersome and unwieldy. Stigmatypes speaks both to the classifying impulse—the impulse to typify—and to the hierarchicalization of categories through denigration of the other. Analytically, stigmatype is needed for another reason: stereotypes need not be stigmatizing." Matt Wray, ed., *Not Quite White* (Durham, NC: Duke University Press, 2006).

38. https://horroraddicts.wordpress.com/2016/02/10/genesis-the-first-black-horror-writersstorytellers-by-linda-addison/.

39. Ibid.

40. Bonnie J. Barthold, *Black Time: Fiction of Africa, the Caribbean, and the United States* (New Haven, CT: Yale University Press, 1981), 3.

Chapter 1. The Importance of Neglected Intersections

1. Yolanda Hood and Gwendolyn D. Pough, "Speculative Black Women: Magic, Fantasy, and the Supernatural," *Femspec* 6, no. 1 (2005).

2. Bly, 2014, #700.

3. Carol J. Clover, *Men, Women and Chainsaws: Gender in the Modern Horror Film* (Princeton, NJ: Princeton University Press, 1992), 13.

4. Natasha Patterson, "Cannibalizing Gender and Genre: A Feminist Re-Vision of George Romero's Zombie Films," in *Zombie Culture: Autopsies of the Living Dead*, ed. Shawn McIntosh and Marc Leverette (Toronto: Scarecrow Press, 2008), 106.

5. bell hooks, "The Oppositional Gaze: Black Female Spectators," in *Feminist Film Theory: A Reader*, ed. Sue Thornham (New York: New York

University Press, 1999,) 314. Clover does include some raced criticism of horror, particularly in the second chapter, "Opening Up," where she creates and names the problematic horror binary of White Science and Black Magic common in contemporary horror films. Though race is included, I deem her use of blackness faulty in that it is employed to create a critical framework that continues to privilege the journey and experiences of the white characters she chooses to examine. Her flirtation with race, and blackness in particular, becomes tangential, for it exists only to assure the survival of the central white character, who must adopt the wisdom of blackness while eschewing the trauma and sociocultural baggage that informs those black epistemologies.

6. Brigid Cherry, *Horror* (New York: Routledge Film Guidebooks, 2009), 176.

7. Clover, *Men, Women and Chainsaws*, 37.

8. Cherry, *Horror*, 174.

9. Clover, *Men, Women and Chainsaws*, 40.

10. Judith Halberstam, *Female Masculinity* (Durham, NC: Duke University Press, 1998), 228.

11. Calvin Hernton, *Sex and Racism in America* (New York: Grove Press, 1966), 38.

12. Hortense Spillers, "Mama's Baby, Papa's Maybe: An American Grammar Book," *Diacritics: A Review of Contemporary Criticism* 17, no. 2 (1987): 65–81.

13. Clover, *Men, Women and Chainsaws*, 45.

14. Ibid., 144.

15. Ibid.

16. Patterson, "Cannibalizing Gender and Genre," 111.

17. Ibid., 106.

18. Ibid., 113.

19. Ibid.

20. hooks, "Oppositional Gaze," 314.

21. See Carol Clover, Barbara Creed, Judith Halberstam, Isabel Cristina Piñedo, and Sue Short.

22. See Harry M. Benshoff, Elizabeth Young, William Shakespeare, Ed Guerrero, and Andrew Curran.

23. See also Richard Dyer, "The Role of Stereotypes," *Media Studies: A Reader* (2000): 245–51.

24. hooks, "Oppositional Gaze," 309.

25. Annalee Newitz, *Pretend We're Dead: Capitalist Monsters in American Pop Culture* (Durham, NC: Duke University Press, 2006), 105.

26. Ibid. 110–11.

27. Harry M. Benshoff, "Blaxploitation Horror Films: Generic Reappropriation or Reinscription?," *Cinema Journal* 39, no. 2 (2000): 31–50.

28. Ibid., 33.

29. Ibid., 38.

30. Ibid., 39.

31. Ibid., 31.

32. Michele Wallace, *Black Macho and the Myth of the Superwoman* (New York: Dial Press, 1979), 107.

33. Tamara Beauboeuf-Lafontant, "Keeping Up Appearances, Getting Fed Up: The Embodiment of Strength among African American Women," *Meridians: Feminism, Race, Transnationalism* 5, no. 2 (2005): 104–23.

34. Ibid., 105.

35. Zora Neale Hurston, *Their Eyes Were Watching God* (Greenwich, CT: Fawcett, 1937).

36. Trudier Harris, "This Disease Called Strength: Some Observations on the Compensating Construction of Black Female Character," *Literature and Medicine* 14, no. 1 (1995): 109–26.

37. Beauboeuf-Lafontant, "Keeping Up Appearances," 32.

38. This difference is highlighted against Sugar's everyday professional style, which is relaxed and more European in styling and texture (Benshoff, "Blaxploitation Horror Films," 31).

39. Robin R. Means Coleman racially genders the "final girl" in *Horror Noire: Blacks in American Horror Films from the 1890s to Present* (2011) with the archetype she refers to as "The Enduring Woman." Means Coleman similarly revises the problematic nature of the strong black woman but limits her readings to 1970s black horror films. The Enduring Woman is often highly sexualized, fights on behalf of her man as well as her own life, and, most important, fights against the boogeymen of racism and corruption.

40. See Barbara Welter, "The Cult of True Womanhood: 1820–1860," *American Quarterly* 18, no. 2 (1966): 151–74.

41. Hazel V. Carby, *Reconstructing Womanhood: The Emergence of the Afro-American Woman Novelist* (New York: Oxford University Press, 1987), 23.

42. Ibid.

43. Ibid., 32.

44. "Looking back" is a purposeful conflation of bell hooks's theories of "talking back" and "the oppositional gaze."

45. hooks, "Oppositional Gaze," 307.

46. The Urban Dictionary defines the eye-fuck as "to look at someone in a deliberately threatening or hostile manner." www.urbandictionary.com.

47. hooks, "Oppositional Gaze," 307.

48. Ibid., 308.

49. Ibid.

50. Ibid.; Donald Bogle, *Toms, Coons, Mulattoes, Mammies, & Bucks: An Interpretive History of Blacks in American Films* (New York: Bloomsbury Publishing, 2001).

51. hooks, "Oppositional Gaze," 316.

52. Ibid., 308.

53. Ibid., 312.

54. Ibid., 316.

55. Though *28 Days Later* (2002) and *The Walking Dead* (2003) contain white males as their central characters, both texts feature significant black female characters, which I would refer to as costars, for their stories develop into central plot points.

56. Linda Williams, "When the Woman Looks," in *Re-vision: Essays in Feminist Film Criticism*, ed. Mary Anne Doane, Patricia Mellencamp, and Linda Williams (Frederick, MD: University Publications of America, 1984), 62.

57. Cherry, *Horror*, 176; Benshoff, "Blaxploitation Horror Films," 32.

58. Patricia Hill Collins defines disjunctures as those small gaps of time and interstitiality—early morning before a family wakes up or late at night once they have gone to bed—when motherwork (the work a mother must do in order to ensure the success and preparation of her family) gets done. I expand Collins's definition of disjunctures to include those gaps in narrative and/or image that contain subversive potential when applying the *oppositional gaze* and use it interchangeably with hooks's own term, "ruptures."

59. Patterson, "Cannibalizing Gender and Genre," 113.

60. In her book *Recreational Terror: Women and the Pleasures of Horror Film Viewing* (Albany: State University Press of New York, 1997), Isabel Cristina Piñedo gives a detailed account of the five characteristics that construct what she defines as "postmodern horror," which include a violent disruption of the everyday world; a transgression and violation of boundaries; the validity of rationality is thrown into question; there is no narrative closure; and the film produces a bounded experience of fear.

61. I only examine Kirkman's *initial* construction of Michonne. *The Walking Dead* is an ongoing comic book series that proves popular as it continues even at the writing of this book. Trade paperbacks 4–6 concern her construction as a raced example of Clover's rape-revenge protagonist, a classic horror trope that is presented within this zombie text. Michonne eventually becomes a more complex character, as Kirkman takes ample advantage of the slow character building that comic book structure allows its creators. Still, I insist that Michonne's introduction to the series is particularly problematic in the sociocultural context of black women and aids in my reimagining of Clover's horror trope.

62. The Governor is the ruthless leader of a parallel group of survivors located in Woodbury, Georgia. He sees other groups of survivors as enemies, particularly when they fail to operate under his dictatorship. He tortures Rick, Glenn, and Michonne to glean information about the prison their band of survivors currently occupies.

63. Tamara Beauboeuf-Lafontant, "You Have to Show Strength: An Exploration of Gender, Race, and Depression," *Gender & Society* 21, no. 1 (2007): 28–51.

64. Beauboeuf-Lafontant, "Keeping Up Appearances," 106.

65. Robert Kirkman, Charlie Adlard, and Cliff Rathburn, *The Walking Dead*, vol. 4, *The Heart's Desire* (Berkeley, CA: Image Comics, 2005).

66. Ibid.

67. At this point in the story, Michonne is the only woman of color.

68. Kirkman, Adlard, and Rathburn, *Heart's Desire*.

69. Ibid.

70. Robert Kirkman, Charlie Adlard, and Cliff Rathburn, *The Walking Dead*, vol. 5, *The Best Defense* (Berkeley, CA: Image Comics, 2006).

71. Carby, *Reconstructing Womanhood*, 16.

72. Kirkman, Adlard, and Rathburn, *Best Defense*.

73. Dorri R. Beam, *Style, Gender, and Fantasy in Nineteenth-Century American Women's Writing* (New York: Cambridge University Press, 2010), 177.

74. Carla Peterson, *"Doers of the Word": African American Women Speakers and Writers in the North (1830–1880)* (New York: Oxford University Press, 1995), 17.

75. Ibid.

76. Carby, *Reconstructing Womanhood*, 24.

77. Robert Kirkman, Charlie Adlard, and Cliff Rathburn, *The Walking Dead*, vol. 6, *This Sorrowful Life* (Berkeley, CA: Image Comics, 2007).

78. Ibid.

79. Ibid.

80. The powerhouse publishers of the comic book industry have always been and continue to be DC Comics and Marvel Comics.

Chapter 2. Black Feminism and the Struggle for Literary Respectability

1. I use the term "literary theory" in a sense that is textually inclusive. I expand beyond novels and short stories to include film, comic books, graphic novels, and so forth.

2. S. Jackson, "Terrans, Extraterrestrials, Warriors and the Last (Wo)man Standing," *African Identities* 7 no. 2 (May 2009): 237–53; Susana M. Morris, "Black Girls Are from the Future: Afrofuturist Feminism in Octavia E. Butler's Fledgling," *WSQ: Women's Studies Quarterly* 40 nos. 3–4 (Fall/Winter 2012): 146–66; Gina Wisker, "Your Buried Ghosts Have a Way of Tripping You Up: Revisioning and Mothering in African-American and Afro-Caribbean Women's Speculative Horror," *Femspec* 6, no. 1 (June 2005): 71–81.

3. Hazel V. Carby, *Reconstructing Womanhood: The Emergence of the Afro-American Woman Novelist* (New York: Oxford University Press, 1987), 4.

4. Patricia Hill Collins, *Black Feminist Thought: Knowledge, Consciousness, and the Politics of Empowerment* (New York: Routledge, 1990), 22.

5. There are, of course, many outliers of black feminist theory outside of this almost twenty-year period—for example, Mary McLeod Bethune,

Kimberly Crenshaw, and others. For my critical purposes, I focus on this incredibly productive period when contemporary black feminist theory began articulating and fighting for its identity.

6. Critic Hazel V. Carby describes herself writing within the "black women's renaissance," marked by "the contemporary discovery and recognition of black women by the corporate world of academia, publishing, and Hollywood" as well as the celebrity status of Alice Walker and Toni Morrison. (Carby, *Reconstructing*, 7).

7. Gloria T. Hull, Patricia Bell Scott, and Barbara Smith, eds., *All the Women Are White, All the Blacks Are Men: But Some of Us Are Brave: Black Women's Studies* (New York: Feminist Press at CUNY, 1993), xviii.

8. Deborah E. McDowell, "New Directions for Black Feminist Criticism," *Black American Literature Forum* 14 (1980): 153–59. For brevity's sake, I am presenting a somewhat reductive articulation on black feminist theory. Black feminist theory has also conducted excellent work on how black women's sexuality and class status have also worked as oppressive identities.

9. Carby, *Reconstructing Womanhood*, 8.

10. See Barbara Christian's later essays, such as "Diminishing Returns: Can Black Feminism Survive the Academy? (1994)" in *New Black Feminist Criticism, 1985–2000*. Ed. Gloria Bowles, M. Giulia Fahi, and Arlene Keizer (Champaign: University of Illinois Press, 2010).

11. I acknowledge that the culling and differentiation of the more academically esteemed label of literature from the sea of fiction writing are primary tasks of the literary critic. I also recognize that multiple parameters are applied when bestowing this title that move beyond the quality of the writing. Timeliness of its themes, availability of texts, and being published in certain languages and by certain publishers are all measurements of the "worthiness" of literature that are subject to political machinations. My critique concerns itself with all of these different influences.

12. Deborah Gray White, *Too Heavy a Load: Black Women in Defense of Themselves, 1894–1994* (New York: W. W. Norton, 1999), 24.

13. Qtd. in ibid., 23.

14. Qtd. in ibid., 21.

15. Qtd. in ibid., 48.

16. This practice is in direct contrast to the patriarchal notions of classic literature, particularly the idea that an author must metaphorically kill and separate himself from his literary forefathers, disavowing their literary influences. Critic Harold Bloom defines this complicated relationship in *The Anxiety of Influence: A Theory of Poetry* (Oxford: Oxford University Press, 1973). The most well known example in African American literature remains the complex literary relationships between Richard Wright and his literary forefather, Ralph Ellison, as well as his literary descendent, James Baldwin.

17. Pages 73–158 feature excerpts and critical contextualization on Harper's *Iola Leroy* (1892), "Sappho" from her novel *Contending Forces* (1900), "Bro'r Abr'm Jimson's Wedding: A Christmas Story (1901) by Hopkins, and Williams's "The Colored Girl" (1905).

18. Mary Helen Washington, *Invented Lives: Narratives of Black Women 1860–1960* (Rockland, MA: Anchor Press, 1987), 75–76.

19. Barbara Christian, *Black Women Novelists: The Development of a Tradition, 1892–1976* (Santa Barbara, CA: Praeger: 1980), 5.

20. These are only a few of the leading scholars who took up the burden of literary race work. This list is not exhaustive. I mention other leading black feminist literary scholars throughout this section.

21. Stephanie J. Shaw, *What a Woman Ought to Be and to Do: Black Professional Women Workers during the Jim Crow Era* (Chicago: University of Chicago Press, 2010), 14.

22. Barbara Smith, "Toward a Black Feminist Criticism," in *African American Literary Theory: A Reader*, ed. Winston Napier (New York: New York University Press, 2000), 159.

23. Ibid., 160.

24. Ibid., 159.

25. Barbara Christian, "But What Do We Think We're Doing Anyway: The State of Black Feminist Criticism or My Version of a Little Bit of History (1989)," in *New Black Feminist Criticism*, 10.

26. Ibid., 11.

27. Ibid., 16.

28. Ibid., 13–14.

29. Barbara Christian, "Whose Canon Is It Anyway? (1994)," in *New Black Feminist Criticism*, 186.

30. Barbara Christian, "Diminishing Returns: Can Black Feminism Survive the Academy? (1994)," in *New Black Feminist Criticism*, 215.

31. It is necessary to note that my assertions remain limited to the beliefs and actions of Barbara Christian and her critical black feminist legacy. Some black feminist scholars have never shied away from the speculative nature of black feminist writing. For example, Trudier Harris's insistence upon reading black women's writing through a folkloric framework has allowed her to wrestle with the speculative and the supernatural throughout her criticism. See *Fiction and Folklore: The Novels of Toni Morrison* (1993) and *The Power of the Porch: The Storyteller's Craft in Zora Neale Hurston, Gloria Naylor, and Randall Kenan* (1996).

32. Email conversation with Mae G. Henderson, August 21, 2013.

33. Jewelle Gomez, "Speculative Fiction and Black Lesbians," *Signs: Theorizing Lesbian Experience* 18, no. 4 (1993): 952.

34. Ibid., 950.

35. Jewelle Gomez, interview by author, spring 2014.

36. There has since been an onslaught of criticism concerning Octavia Butler and her work. I am limiting my critique to the peak of black feminist theory's creation I set earlier in the chapter, the late 1970s to early 1990s.

37. Charles R. Saunders, "Why Blacks Should Read (and Write) Science Fiction," *American Visions* 15, no. 5 (2000): 399–400.

38. Ibid., 400.

39. Gomez, "Speculative Fiction and Black Lesbians," 951.

40. A full analysis of Gloria Naylor's *Mama Day* (1988) can be found in chapter 4 of this text.

41. Alberto Ríos, "Magical Realism: Definitions," http://www.public.asu.edu/~aarios/resourcebank/definitions/.

42. Saunders, "Why Blacks Should Read (and Write) Science Fiction," 400.

43. Christian, "Diminishing Returns," 215.

Chapter 3. Black Women Writing Fluid Fiction

1. See Cheryl Walls's concept of "worrying the lines" in this book's introduction, note 3.

2. The genre definitions I have chosen to use are not perfect—none of them are. I have chosen the Library of Congress's definitions as

generalizations to move this conversation on genre confusion forward and bring in other critics.

3. Library of Congress, Humanities and Social Sciences Division, "Library of Congress Policy Statements: Fantasy and Science Fiction," ed. Library of Congress (Washington, DC: Library of Congress, 2008), 8.

4. Robin Wood, "Return of the Repressed," *Film Comment* 14, no. 4 (1978): 25.

5. Library of Congress, Humanities and Social Sciences Division, "Library of Congress Policy Statements: Fantasy and Science Fiction," 2.

6. Ibid.

7. Ibid.

8. Ibid.

9. This reality is reflected in the conflated association of these three genres in critical discussions and popular culture. Many critics and a majority of fans and publishers denote this genre conflation and confusion with the aid of the "/". It is very common to see these genres discussed as science fiction/fantasy/horror, S/F/F, and even SFF. I at times use this shorthand to illuminate the genres' entanglement with each other.

10. Serling also wrote the original screenplay of *Planet of the Apes* (1968).

11. Clarke is broadly considered one of the fathers of contemporary science fiction and the icon who cowrote *2001: A Space Odyssey*, a foundational science fiction film adapted from the manuscript of his 1968 novel of the same name.

12. *2001: A Space Odyssey* (1968).

13. Ibid.

14. Arthur C. Clarke, *Profiles of the Future: An Inquiry into the Limits of the Possible* (New York: Bantam Books, 1967).

15. John Clute and John Grant, "Encyclopedia of Fantasy: Introduction to the Online Text," in *Encyclopedia of Fantasy*, ed. John Clute and John Grant (London: Orbit, 1997).

16. Edward James and Farah Mendlesohn, eds., *The Cambridge Companion to Fantasy Literature* (Cambridge: Cambridge University Press, 2012), 1.

17. Ibid.

18. Sylvia Kelso, "Out of Egypt: Histories of Speculative Fiction and Carole McDonnell's *Wind Follower*," *Extrapolation* 51, no. 1 (2010): 84.

19. Clute and Grant, "Encyclopedia of Fantasy."

20. Ibid.

21. Ibid.

22. Ibid.

23. Ibid.

24. Gwendolyn D. Pough, and Yolanda Hood, "Speculative Black Women: Magic, Fantasy, and the Supernatural," *Femspec* 6, no. 1 (2005): ix.

25. Robert A. Heinlein, "On the Writing of Speculative Fiction" (1947), 138–56.

26. Speculative fiction truly is everywhere. The Speculative Literature Foundation (speculativeliterature.org) appeals to critics and authors by offering grants, fellowships, and awards as well as links to publishers and writing workshops. *Strange Horizons* is a weekly e-magazine that acts as a trade magazine as well as publishing the best new literatures. Finally, there exists isfdb.org, or *The Internet Speculative Fiction Database*.

27. N. E. Lilly, "What Is Speculative Fiction?" *Green Tentacles*, March 2002, http://www.greententacles.com/articles/5/26/.

28. Susana M. Morris, "Black Girls Are from the Future: Afrofuturist Feminism in Octavia Butler's *Fledgling*," *WSQ: Women's Studies Quarterly* 40 (Fall/Winter 2012): 152.

29. David Wyatt, "Speculative Fiction," December 10, 2007/March 29, 2014, http://www.contextsf.org/blog/2007/12/speculative-fiction.html.

30. Gregory E. Rutledge and Nalo Hopkinson, "Speaking in Tongues: An Interview with Science Fiction Writer Nalo Hopkinson," *African American Review* 33, no. 4 (1999): 589.

31. Pough and Hood, "Speculative Black Women."

32. Ibid., xi.

33. Ibid.

34. Patricia Hill Collins. *Black Feminist Thought: Knowledge, Consciousness and the Politics of Empowerment* (New York: Routledge, 2002). I purposely conflate past, present, and future, for I insist that the fluid nature of black women's genre writing collapses and rejects the supposed linear nature of time. The African influence of these women's works perpetuates the West African ideal of Sankofa—in which the past, present, and future are equally important and exist as one.

35. Nnedi Okorafor, "Organic Fantasy," *African Identities* 7, no. 2 (2009): 277.

36. Sandra Jackson and Julie Moody-Freeman, "The Genre of Science Fiction and the Black Imagination," *African Identities* 7, no. 2 (2009): 128.

Jackson and Moody-Freeman begin their editorial note by successfully explicating the nuances of speculative fiction. Unfortunately, toward the end, the editors begin to conflate science fiction, fantasy, and speculative fiction into one umbrella term, science fiction, for the rest of their journal issue. Their problematic—yet wholly understandable—decision supports my contention that many of the aforementioned terms, especially speculative fiction, fail to address the particular needs of black women genre writers.

37. Ibid., 129.

38. Mark Dery, "Black to the Future: Interviews with Samuel R. Delany, Greg Tate, and Tricia Rose," *South Atlantic Quarterly* 92, no. 4 (1993): 735 (emphasis added).

39. Mark Sinker, "Loving the Alien in Advance of the Landing—Black Science Fiction," *WIRE* 96 (February 1992).

40. Dery, "Black to the Future," 735.

41. Ibid.

42. Ancient Egypt is certainly not the only African empire that exists in Afrofuturistic writing and visual arts, but there is certainly a heavy preponderance for that time period.

43. Afrofuturism's "problem with the past" is being critically examined by proponents of the framework. Alondra Nelson edited a special volume of the journal *Social Text* centering on "works [that] represent new directions in the study of African diaspora culture that are grounded in the histories of black communities, rather than seeking to sever all connections to them." Nelson and other Afrofuturists are openly expanding the framework's theoretical territory—things are changing. I choose to address the central tenets of Afrofuturism even as I acknowledge its rich contemporary offerings. See Alondra Nelson, "Introduction: Future Texts," *Social Text* 20, no. :2 (2002): 1–15.

44. Kodwo Eshun, "Further Considerations on Afrofuturism," *CR: The New Centennial Review* 3, no. 2 (2003): 293, 294.

45. Marleen S. Barr, ed., *Afro-Future Females: Black Writers Chart Science Fiction's Newest Wave Trajectory* (Columbus: Ohio State University Press, 2008), xv.

46. Mark Bould, "The Ships Landed Long Ago: Afrofuturism and Black SF," *Science Fiction Studies* (2007): 182.

47. bell hooks, "Homeplace: A Site of Resistance," in *Yearning: Race, Gender, and Cultural Politics* (Cambridge, MA: South End Press, 1990).

48. Jewelle Gomez, "The Second Law of Thermodynamics: Transcription of a Panel at the 1997 Black Speculative Fiction Writers Conference Held at Clark Atlanta University," in *Dark Matter: Reading the Bones*, ed. Sheree R. Thomas (Ringgold, GA: Aspect, 2004), 416.

49. Literary respectability politics are the set of paradigms constructed by early black feminist literary theorists to privilege the writings of certain black women authors in order to breach the politics of the academy. See chapter 2.

50. hooks, "Homeplace," 19.

51. Nalo Hopkinson, *Skin Folk* (New York: Aspect, 2001), 223.

52. Patricia Hill Collins explores these issues in-depth in her text *Black Sexual Politics: African Americans, Gender, and the New Racism* (New York: Routledge, 2004).

53. Hopkinson, *Skin Folk*, 240.

54. Ibid., 243.

55. Ibid., 244.

56. Ibid.

57. bell hooks, "The Politics of Radical Black Subjectivity," in *Yearning: Race, Gender, and Cultural Politics*, 20.

58. Ibid., 15.

59. Ibid., 104.

60. Ibid., 21.

61. Nalo Hopkinson, "Introduction," in *So Long Been Dreaming: Postcolonial Science Fiction and Fantasy*, ed. Nalo Hopkinson and Uppinder Mehan (Vancouver, BC: Arsenal Pulp Press, 2004), 8.

62. hooks, "Politics of Radical Black Subjectivity," 15.

63. Patricia Hill Collins, *Black Feminist Thought: Knowledge, Consciousness and the Politics of Empowerment* (New York: Routledge, 1990), 145.

64. Ibid., 148.

65. See the following: Gina Wisker, "Celebrating Difference and Community: The Vampire in African-American and Caribbean Women's Writing," in *Transnational and Postcolonial Vampires: Dark Blood*, ed. Tabish Khair and Johan Höglund (New York: Palgrave Macmillan, 2012), 46–66; Lee Skallerup Bessette, "'They Can Fly': The Postcolonial

Black Body in Nalo Hopkinson's Speculative Short Fiction," in *The Postcolonial Short Story; Contemporary Essays*, ed. Maggie Awadallo and Paul March-Russell (New York: Palgrave Macmillan, 2013), 167–81; Marlene D. Allen, "Tricksterism, Masquerades, and the Legacy of the African Diasporic Past in Nalo Hopkinson's Midnight Robber," in *Afterimages of Slavery: Essays on Appearances in Recent American Films, Literature, Television and Other Media*, ed. Marlene D. Allen and Seretha D. Williams (Jefferson, NC: McFarland, 2012), 76–88.

66. Nalo Hopkinson, "Greedy Choke Puppy," in *Skin Folk* (2001), 174.

67. Ibid., 170.

68. Ibid., 176.

69. Ibid.

70. Ibid., 178.

71. Clarke, *Profiles of the Future*.

72. See Kinitra D. Brooks, *Maternal Inheritances: Trinity Formations and Constructing Self-Identities in Stigmata and Louisiana*, vol. 12 (San Francisco: Femspec, 2012).

73. The female protagonist is never physically described. It is heavily suggested that she is of African descent. Her parents are described as being brown-skinned, and her fiancé is of Nigerian Ibo descent. Also, Butler's well-established precedence for writing black female protagonists in the majority of her works supports my racialized reading of the central character.

74. Octavia Butler, "The Evening and the Morning and the Night," *Callaloo* 24, no. 2 (2001): 401.

75. Ibid., 411.

76. Ibid., 414.

77. Ibid.

78. Hopkinson frequently mentions Octavia Butler as an influence and mentor. Since Butler's death, Hopkinson is one of many who work tirelessly to continue Butler's literary legacy of black women in so-called speculative fiction.

79. Ibid., 402, 409.

80. Ibid., 415.

81. Toni Morrison, *Sula* (New York: Random House, 1998), 174.

82. Though the story collection *Skin Folk* holds a copyright date of 2001, Hopkinson's exposition of Jacky's intellectual success and her incessant

need to measure herself against her lack of domestic success appears almost prescient of the black woman marriage crisis of the early twenty- first century. The public concern trolling of the marriage prospects for successful black women began with the rising prevalence of the Obamas as they were swept into the White House in 2008, solidified with a *Nightline* special in December 2009, and reached a frenzied crescendo in the spring and summer of 2010 as both the *Economist* and the *New York Times* featured articles analyzing the lack of marriage prospects for single educated black women. http://www .feministe.us/blog/archives/2010/06/21/the-media-v-black-women-the- peculiar-case-of-the-media%E2%80%99s-obsession-with-unmarried- black-women/.

83. Nalo Hopkinson, *Skin Folk* (New York: Warner Books, 2001), 180. "Doux-doux" is a Caribbean term of endearment derived from the French. It literally means sweet-sweet and translates to sweetie, sweetheart, or sweetness.

84. These gods are from traditional African religions mostly associated with the Yoruba peoples of West Africa. I also refer to these gods interchangeably as orishas and loas, which are from the Santeria and Vodou traditions, respectively. I do this as an acknowledgment of Hopkinson's purposeful use of the Yoruban traditions as they mani- fested in the New World through the religious practices of enslaved Africans who wisely blended their worship practices with the Catholicism/Christianity of their Spanish (Santeria) and French (Vodou) enslavers. These were the peoples that populated the Caribbean, and it is their traditions and their foundational cultural influences that Hopkinson repeatedly and openly acknowledges in her works.

85. Nalo Hopkinson, *Sister Mine* (New York: Hachette, 2013).

86. Ibid., 42.

87. Margarite Fernández Olmos and Lizabeth Paravisini-Gebert, *Creole Religions of the Caribbean: An Introduction from Vodou and Santeria to Obeah and Espiritismo* (New York: New York University Press, 2003), 117.

88. Hopkinson, *Sister Mine*, 29.

89. Olmos and Paravisini-Gebert, *Creole Religions of the Caribbean*, 39.

90. Ibid., 120. There are multiple manifestations of Vodou in Africa and its diaspora. I focus my readings of Vodou in Hopkinson's work, specifically on Haitian Vodou—with some deviation into New Orleans Vodou, which is incredibly similar.

91. Ibid. Lwa and loa are interchangeable and simply different spellings of the same verbal sound (low-ah) and concept. This is because Haitian Creole or patois owes it origins to its oral culture and not the written word; therefore, spellings of the loas contain some variation across different parts of Haiti and are manifested in the texts associated with Vodou. From phone interview with Jude Michel, Vodou Mambo or priestess, practicing over fifteen years, on April 8, 2013.

92. http://www.viking-mythology.com/yggdrasil.php.

93. Rutledge and Hopkinson, "Speaking in Tongues," 592.

94. Hopkinson, *Sister Mine*, 95.

95. http://santeriachurch.org/the-orishas/yemaya/.

96. Hopkinson, *Sister Mine*, 98.

97. Ibid., 32.

98. Ibid., 69.

99. Mambo Chita Tann, *Haitian Vodou: An Introduction to Haiti's Indigenous Spiritual Tradition* (Woodbury, MN: Llewellyn Worldwide, 2012), 103.

100. http://santeriachurch.org/the-orishas/orisha-oko/.

101. Hopkinson, *Sister Mine*, 32.

102. http://santeriachurch.org/the-orishas/eleggua/.

103. Hopkinson, *Sister Mine*, 98.

104. Baron Samedi is a well-known popular cultural figure. Baron Samedi has featured prominently in the James Bond film *Live and Let Die* (1973), as portrayed by Geoffrey Holder. Dr. Facilier, the villain in Disney's *The Princess and the Frog* (2009), is a watered-down version of Baron Samedi, so he is more palatable for a children's film. Baron Samedi also features prominently in the fifth season, episode nineteen, of the television series *Supernatural* (2005–), titled "Hammer of the Gods."

105. http://santeriachurch.org/the-orishas/eleggua/.

106. Hopkinson, *Sister Mine*, 94. A Kalashnikov is the name given to a series of assault rifles invented by Soviet Mikhail Kalashnikov just after World War II. The most popular Kalashnikov weapon is the AK-47. See http://www.militaryfactory.com/smallarms/kalashnikov-guns.asp for more information.

107. http://santeriachurch.org/the-orishas/ogun/.

108. Ibid.

109. Hopkinson, *Sister Mine*, 97.

110. Ibid., 98.

111. Ochosi and Ogun are the best of friends—along with Eleggua, the three are considered inseparable. Along with the orisha Osun, the four orishas are "The Warriors"—"one of the initiations a person receives making him an Aborish or worshipper of the orishas. [Eleggua], Ogun, and Ochosi work together to help a person's spiritual development. Eleggua opens the road, Ogun clears it and Ochosi helps that person attain their goal as easily as possible, like the straight shot of his arrow." http://santeriachurch.org/the-orishas/ochosi/.

112. Ibid.

113. Hopkinson, *Sister Mine*, 98.

114. http://santeriachurch.org/the-orishas/ogun/.

115. Hopkinson, *Sister Mine*, 98.

116. Henry Louis Gates Jr. *The Signifying Monkey: A Theory of African-American Literary Criticism* (New York: Oxford University Press, 1988), 30.

117. Nnedi Okorafor, "Organic Fantasy," *African Identities* 7 no. 2 (May 2009): 278.

118. Ibid.

119. Rutledge and Hopkinson, "Speaking in Tongues," 592–93.

120. Hopkinson, *Sister Mine*, 57.

121. Ibid.

122. Marshall, Paule. "From the Poets in the Kitchen." *Callaloo* 18 (1983): 22–30.

123. Rutledge and Hopkinson, "Speaking in Tongues," 600.

124. Marshall, "From the Poets in the Kitchen," 50.

125. Ibid., 50.

126. Rutledge and Hopkinson, "Speaking in Tongues," 601.

Chapter 4. Folkloric Horror

1. Scholar Teresa N. Washington refers to Àjé (ashe) as a spiritual life force thst is divinely female in its source. Teresa N. Washington, *Our Mothers, Our Powers, Our Texts: Manifestations of Àjé in Africana literature* (Bloomington: Indiana University Press, 2005), 3–16.

2. The ghede are the spirits of the dead from the Haitian Vodoun tradition. They are celebrated annually during Fete Ghede, a religious holiday that acknowledges the power and the presence of the dead in the daily lives of African diasporic peoples.

3. Lene Brøndum, "'The Persistence of Tradition': The Retelling of Sea Islands Culture in Works by Julie Dash, Gloria Naylor, and Paule Marshall," in *Black Imagination and the Middle Passage* (Oxford: Oxford University Press, 1999), 153–163 (qtd. in Venetria K. Patton's *The Grasp That Reaches Beyond the Grave*).

4. Venetria K. Patton, *The Grasp That Reaches Beyond the Grave: The Ancestral Call in Black Women's Texts* (Albany, NY: SUNY Press, 2013), 9.

5. The Bram Stoker Award is given by the Horror Writers Association and is awarded each year at the World Horror Convention.

6. I would like to reiterate that both of these successful writers enthusiastically support and mentor rising black women genre/horror writers.

7. "We must learn how to see." bell hooks, *Yearning: Race, Gender, and Cultural Politics* (Cambridge, MA: South End Press, 1990), 111–12.

8. http://sumikosaulson.com/2013/02/12/20-black-women-in-horror-writing/.

9. http://sumikosaulson.com/2013/02/18/10-more-black-women-in-horror-fiction/ as well as http://sumikosaulson.com/2014/02/19/nineteen-more-black-women-in-horror-writing-list-3/.

10. http://www.amazon.com/60-Black-Women-Horror-Fiction/dp/1496112946.

11. http://www.graveyardshiftsisters.com/p/mission.html.

12. "Magical Realism," Oxford Reference Online, http://www.oxfordreference.com.libweb.lib.utsa.edu/view/10.1093/acref/9780199532919.001.0001/acref-9780199532919-e-422?rskey=ogJoCN&result=1.

13. "Just as long as they don't call me a magical realist, as though I don't have a culture to write out of. As though that culture has no intellect." "Living Memory: A Meeting with Toni Morrison," Black Atlantic Exchanges, 181.

14. http://www.graveyardshiftsisters.com/2014/12/on-our-terms-black-woman-horror-film.html.

15. Ibid.

16. hooks, *Yearning*, 164.

17. Ibid., 166.

18. Ibid., 174.

19. Ibid., 172.

20. Nnedi Okorafor, "Organic Fantasy," *African Identities* 7, no. 2 (2009): 275–86.

21. Gwendolyn D. Pough and Yolanda Hood. "Speculative Black Women: Magic, Fantasy, and the Supernatural," *Femspec* 6, no. 1 (2005).

22. Ibid., 4

23. For an example of the problematic ways in which mainstream horror texts treat traditional African religions, see the following books and films: *White Zombie* (1932); *I Walked with a Zombie* (1943) dir. Jacques Tourneur; *Darkfall* (1984) by Dean Koontz; *The Serpent and the Rainbow* (1988) dir. Wes Craven; *The Believers* (1987) dir. John Schlesinger; *Angel Heart* (1987) dir. Alan Parker. A contemporary film that is subversive to this tradition is Kate Hudson's 2005 vehicle, *The Skeleton Key* dir. Iain Softley.

24. John S. Mbiti, *African Religions and Philosophy* (Gaborone, Botswana: Heinemann Education Botswana, 1969), 79.

25. Ibid., 82.

26. Patton, *Grasp That Reaches Beyond the Grave*, 17.

27. Ibid., 16.

28. Ibid.

29. Kinitra D. Brooks, "Maternal Inheritances: Trinity Formations and Constructing Self-identities in Stigmata and Louisiana," *Femspec* 12, no. 2 (2012): 19–58.

30. The practice of dressing in all-white is derived from the Yoruban religious practice of Ifa. It also has passed down to syncretized versions of Ifa—Santeria, Vodoun, and Candomble. Practitioners are expected to wear white during different ceremonies and as they perform certain cleansings/limpias.

31. A female priestess of Vodou is a called a Mambo, while an advanced female practitioner/priestess of Santeria is a Santera, and an Obeah woman practices obeah, a spiritual practice established in Jamaica with a foundation in traditional African religions.

32. Interview with Arek Samuels, practitioner, June 11, 2016.

33. http://santeriachurch.org/our-services/santeria-initiations/.

34. Some versions of "Chocolate Park" also contain a white family struggling in the tenement. I choose not to examine this family for my analysis and focus upon Lady Black.

35. Lady Black is originally from Haiti. I suspect she works with the hot/ Petro/Petwo loas of Haitian Vodou.

36. Lady Black's flashing red eyes solidify my assertion that she is a practitioner of Haitian Vodou. Erzulie Red Eyes, a manifestation of the loa Erzulie Dantor, is a spirit of feminine vengeance.

37. Again, I suspect New Orleans Vodou. The story takes place in New Orleans, and Rosamojo is known to wear what is often referred to as a gris-gris bag, a small bag containing protective objects and blessings unique to the wearer, around her neck.

38. Kiini Ibura Salaam, "Rosamojo," *Ancient, Ancient* (Seattle, WA: Aqueduct Press, 2012), Location 1371.

39. Ibid., 1384.

40. Mbiti, *African Religions and Philosophy*, 78.

41. Ibid., 78–79.

42. "Blues and sacred music are joined at the hip. Most blues musicians grow up in the church where as children they learn to sing hymns and spirituals. One blues musician told me that if a singer wants to cross over from sacred music to the blues, he simply replaces 'my God' with 'my baby' and continues singing the same song." William Ferris, *Give My Poor Heart Ease: Voices of the Mississippi Blues* (Chapel Hill: University of North Carolina Press, 2009).

43. Yvonne P. Chireau, *Black Magic: Religion and the African American Conjuring Tradition* (Berkeley: University of California Press, 2006), 12.

44. Trudier Harris, *Fiction and Folklore: The Novels of Toni Morrison* (Knoxville: University of Tennessee Press, 1991), 2–3.

45. Kameelah L. Martin, *Conjuring Moments in African American Literature: Women, Spirit Work, and Other Such Hoodoo* (New York: Palgrave Macmillan, 2012), 1–2.

46. Harris, *Fiction and Folklore*, 3.

47. Martin, *Conjuring Moments in African American Literature*, 161.

48. Chireau, *Black Magic*, 23, 24.

49. Angela Y. Davis, *Blues Legacies and Black Feminism: Gertrude "Ma" Rainey, Bessie Smith, and Billie Holiday* (New York: Vintage Books, 1998), 5.

50. Ibid., 6.

51. Ibid., 6, 8.

52. Chireau, *Black Magic*, 147, 148, 150 (emphasis added).

53. Ibid., 148.

54. Martin, *Conjuring Moments in African American Literature*, 128.

55. Ibid.

56. Chireau, *Black Magic*, 145; Davis, *Blues Legacies and Black Feminism*, 128.

57. Martin, *Conjuring Moments in African American Literature*, see chapter 4, "Of Blues Narratives and Conjure Magic: A Symbiotic Dialectic."

58. Farah Jasmine Griffin, "When Malindy Sings: A Meditation on Black Women's Vocality," in *Uptown Conversation: The New Jazz Studies*, ed. Robert O'Meally and Farah Jasmine Griffin (New York: Columbia University Press, 2012), 110.

59. Davis, *Blues Legacies and Black Feminism*, 11.

60. Ibid., 13.

61. Ibid.

62. Chireau, *Black Magic*, 24.

63. Paul Garon and Beth Garon, *Woman with Guitar: Memphis Minnie's Blues* (New York: Da Capo Press, 1992), 45.

64. Chireau, *Black Magic*, 140.

65. Ibid., 147.

66. Davis, *Blues Legacies and Black Feminism*, 130.

67. Daphne Brooks, *Bodies in Dissent: Spectacular Performances of Race and Freedom, 1850–1910* (Durham, NC: Duke University Press, 2006), 3.

68. Garon and Garon, *Woman with Guitar*, 5.

69. For more information on the distinction between these blues eras—as well as the complex gender politics it represents—see Hazel V. Carby's "It Just Be's Dat Way Sometime: The Sexual Politics of Women's Blues" (1986), Paul and Beth Garon's *Woman with Guitar: Memphis Minnie's Blues* (1992), and Steven C. Tracy's "To the Tune of Those Weary Blues: The Influence of the Blues Tradition in Langston Hughes's Blues Poems" (1981).

70. Garon and Garon, *Woman with Guitar*, 99.

71. See ibid., 50–53, as the authors describe the process of divining Memphis Minnie as the writer and composer of all of her songs. Minnie lists her

second husband on all of her later copyrights, but as an apparent peace offering for her atypical economic and temperamental independence.

72. Ibid., 45.

73. Ibid., 22.

74. Ibid.

75. Gabriel Solis's talk at AstroBlackness 2: The Surreal, The Speculative, and The Spooky, Loyola Marymount University, March 12–13, 2015.

76. Langston Hughes, "Here to Yonder," in *PL Jazzbook* (1947).

77. Daphne A. Brooks, "Nina Simone's Triple Play," *Callalo* 34, no. 3 (Winter 2011): 181.

78. Danielle C. Heard, "'Don't Let Me Be Misunderstood': Nina Simone's Theater of Invisibility," *Callaloo* 35, no. 4 (Fall 2012): 1057.

79. Melanie E. Bratcher, *Words and Songs of Bessie Smith, Billie Holiday, and Nina Simone: Sound Motion, Blues Spirit, and African Memory*, 1st ed. (London: Taylor and Francis, 2007).

80. https://www.youtube.com/watch?v=9jicLmH8tlU.

81. *What Happened, Miss Simone?*, dir. Liz Garbus. Netflix, 2015.

82. Legend has it that Hawkins recorded the outrageous version of the song while being "blackout drunk" at the behest of his producer, Maxim. Multiple articles cite a 1991 *Los Angeles Times* interview with Hawkins. Unfortunately, the short *Times* interview does not mention this particular story.

83. Musicologist Gabriel Solis's remarks are taken from his talk at Astro Blackness 2 on the panel "I'll Put a Spell On You: The Supernatural in Black Music." Solis names Simone's live performances of "I'll Put a Spell On You" as "incredibly subversive" as compared to the recorded version. My argument pushes Solis further by directly naming Simone as a conjure woman in the live performance.

84. Heard, "'Don't Let Me Be Misunderstood,'" 1072.

Conclusion

1. https://mindofmalaka.com/2016/04/25/can-Beyoncé-wear-another-womans-skin-and-still-be-a-feminist-icon/.

2. The reading of this verse using the horror framework of the Boo Hag came about mutually in various conversations with scholar John Jennings.

3. The Gullah people are descendants of West Africans brought to the sea islands of South Carolina and Georgia to be enslaved. They have retained many of their cultural traditions, which are directly linked to West Africa. More information can be found at their official website: https://gullahgeecheenation.com/.

4. "Shift" is a short story that has yet to be officially published. It is due to be published later this year. The author has provided a preview copy of the short story that has yet to be formatted and still exists in Microsoft Word document form.

5. Nalo Hopkinson admits to being "obsessed" with mermaids in a discussion with the author during multiple discussions while attending AstroBlackness 2: The Surreal, The Speculative, and The Spooky at Loyola Marymount University, March 12–13, 2015. In fact, the mermaid/octopus woman figure features prominently on the program schedule—drawn by art and pop culture scholar John Jennings.

6. Scylla and Charybdis are water deities from Greek mythology. Both are considered monstrous, and Scylla, the half-octopus/half-woman, is particularly associated as an early incarnation of the monstrous feminine. Charybdis manifests as a powerful whirlpool. Odysseus confronts both monsters in Homer's *The Odyssey*.

7. Hopkinson, "Shift," 14.

8. Ibid., 14–15.

9. Ibid., 15.

10. Ibid.

Index

haints (hant), 8, 14, 83, 91–92, 130

Haiti, 156–58; language of, 186n91; Vodou in, 85, 186nn90–91, 188n2, 190nn35–36

Harper, Frances E. W., 43, 47; *Iola Leroy*, 47, 178n17

Harris, Trudier, 26, 114–15, 179n31

Hawkins, Jalacy, 124–25, 192n82; "I'll Put a Spell on You," 124–26, 192nn82–83

Heard, Danielle, 124–26

Hood, Yolanda, 16, 66–67, 102

Hoodoo, 104, 108, 114, 117, 143

"Hoodoo Lady" (Minnie), 121–24, 149–50

hooks, bell, 7, 28–29, 74–75, 99, 174n58; and black aesthetics, 75, 113; and homeplace, 71–72; and oppositional gaze, 11, 28–29, 174n44

Hopkinson, Nalo, 66, 72–74, 184n78, 185n84, 193n5; and Afrofuturism, 69; fluid fiction of, 77–94; *The Salt Roads*, 91, 156; *Sister Mine*, 82–94; *Skin Folk*, 77, 91, 147–48, 158–59, 184n82; and Sycorax, 130–32

horror, 1–6, 79, 83, 91–92, 96–98; black women in, 8, 101–2; industry of, 99. *See also* folkloric horror

Horror Noire: Blacks in American Horror Films from the 1890s to Present (Coleman), 12–13, 42, 173n39

Hull, Gloria T., 10, 48

Hundred Thousand Kingdoms, The (Jemisin), 63–65, 150–51

Hurston, Zora Neale, 14, 26, 47, 144–45; *Every Tongue Got to Confess: Negro Folktales from the Gulf States*, 14, 100, 144–45

hybridity, 65, 77

identificatory permeability, 19, 21–22, 26, 30, 32

identity, 11, 19, 21, 44; black women's, 10–11, 26, 75; Caribbean, 77, 85, 93–94; gender, 22; intersections of, 35, 40, 44; multiple, 25–26, 101–2; sexual, 72

"I'll Put a Spell on You" (Hawkins), 124–26, 192nn82–83

Iola Leroy (Harper), 47, 178n17

Jackson, Sandra, 42, 67, 181n36

Jamaica, 77, 108, 130, 152, 189n31

Jemisin, N.K., 63–64, 99; *The Hundred Thousand Kingdoms*, 63–65, 150–51

King, Stephen, 58, 151, 154, 158

Kirkman, Robert, 31–36, 165, 175n61; *The Walking Dead*, 165, 174n55

Kubrick, Stanley, 60, 133; *2001: A Space Odyssey*, 60–61, 64, 133–34, 180n11

Lemonade (Beyoncé), 127–28, 152

literary canon, 14, 45, 47–51, 55, 73

literary respectability, 42, 46–53, 73

Living Blood, The (Due), 99, 134

Louisiana, 104, 147, 152–53, 162, 166

Louisiana (Brodber), 98, 104–10, 152–53

magical realism, 9, 100

majority viewer, 21–22, 30, 32, 170n26

Mama Day (Naylor), 105–10, 153

marriage, 108, 118–19, 184n82

Marshall, Paule, 92–93, 140

Martin, Kameelah L., 114–15, 117–18, 120

masculinity, 20, 25, 33, 35, 37, 70

masculinization, 20, 170n28

Minnie, Memphis, 114, 120–24, 149, 191n71; "Hoodoo Lady," 121–24, 149–50

misogyny, 21, 35

Morrison, Toni, 54, 69, 100, 177n6, 188n13; *Beloved*, 54, 84, 103, 138; *Sula*, 79, 81, 160

mother-daughter relationship, 54, 79, 80

motherwork, 37, 76, 86, 174n58

myths, 25, 36, 58, 62, 79; Caribbean 78, 82; Greek, 138–39, 193n6; Norse, 85; surrounding mermaids, 131; vampire, 78

Naylor, Gloria, 53–55, 108, 110, 153; *Mama Day*, 105–10, 153

Negrophobia, 12, 18

New Orleans, 105, 107, 111, 136, 147; Vodou in, 108, 186n90, 190n37

Newsome, Bree, 95, 97, 164

About the Author

KINITRA D. BROOKS is an associate professor of English at the University of Texas at San Antonio. Her research interests include contemporary African American and Afro-Caribbean literature, black feminism, and horror studies. Her short horror fiction collection *Sycorax's Daughters* was coedited with Susana M. Morris and Linda D. Addison at Cedar Grove Publishing. Currently, she is working on a book-length exploration of the monstrosity and divinity of black women's visual culture tentatively titled *Divinely Monstrous: Black Women Conjuring the Grotesque in Popular Culture.* She is also coediting a volume on black women and horror entitled *Towards a Black Women's Horror Aesthetic: Critical Frameworks*, with Susana M. Morris and Linda Addison. She has published articles in *African American Review*, *Obsidian*, and *Fempsec*.